Rewire Your Confidence

Overcome Self-Doubt, Improve Your Self-Esteem, Act Against Your Fears, and Toughen Up To Own Your Life

By Zoe McKey

zoemckey@gmail.com

zoemckey.com

Thank you for choosing my book! I would like to show my appreciation for the trust you gave me by giving you **FREE GIFT**!

For more information visit www.zoemckey.com

Table of Contents

Chapter 1 – How I Misinterpreted Confidence for Entitlement 8

Chapter 2 – Old vs. New Identity 26

Chapter 3 – Progress 38

Chapter 4 – Break Free from Dishonesty 52

Chapter 5 – Acknowledgement and Acceptance 80

Chapter 6 – Guilt and Shame 98

Chapter 7 - Comparison 126

Chapter 8 - The Destructive Power of Judgment ... 156

Chapter 9 – Positive Reinforcement 170

Chapter 10 - Set Your Goals 186

Closing Thoughts 196

Endnotes 204

Chapter 1 – How I Misinterpreted Confidence for Entitlement

As a kid, I was the consummate daddy's princess; a spoiled kid without many parental boundaries. Possibly as a result of how poorly (some might say excellently) I was spoiled, I was outspoken and fearless—and with those traits came an air of utter self-confidence. My persuasive abilities worked on my parents phenomenally. My mother was busy working, my father was a notorious conflict avoider, and my grandparents were readily complying with each demand I had. Whatever I wanted, I received—my mom gave me things out of guilt for not being in my life, my dad gave me things to make me shut up, and my grandparents, well, I think they just behaved as normal grandparents would. I was not only an only child but also an only grandchild. As you can imagine… I had four adults at my service.

I had a conversation with my mom recently where she proudly said, "You were just so headstrong. It always had to be your way. And we went along with your wishes. You were the center of all the decision-making."

Can you imagine a family where a toddler leads the show?

Oh, Mom. If you knew how much damage your permissive parenting caused me later in life… In fact, ever since I stepped out of my tiny kingdom where I was the princess. I'm sure some of you can identify with what I'm saying. To many of us ex-royalty, there came a point in our lives where we realized that the overly permissive parenting that provided an easy childhood brought us only tears and hardship in our adulthood.

My overly inflated ego and sense of entitlement got its first shock in elementary school. Compared to an average seven- or eight-year-old, I had a developed sense of grandeur and I didn't understand the word "no". This was evident to the outside world. Some kids with lower self-esteem were drawn to me as I seemed confident. But those with a healthy sense of self and a stricter upbringing were avoiding me. Eventually, even my friends started avoiding me as I came off bossy and self-centered.

On one hand, I have been extremely lucky when it comes to my upbringing. I never heard a discouraging word from my parents during my childhood—or in my life since then. They always told me I could succeed in life and get everything I wanted if I were focused, dedicated, and worked hard for it. They never rejected even my silliest ideas. I'm truly grateful for them never cutting my wings.

Not cutting off wings and not enabling the child to be a selfish little brat are not mutually exclusive. I'm sure my parents did their best. They came from a communist country—they lacked bitterly in their youth. It's only natural that they wanted to provide me, a child of early democracy, with everything they didn't get. They had no idea of the harmful effects of such crazy enabling. Even today, when I tell them how their enabling harmed me, before my frontal lobes fully developed and I gained some emotional maturity, they reject my explanations.

"You had the best upbringing, we did the best we could."

I don't doubt the second half of that statement, but the first half is wildly delusional and in denial. But hey, who said in order to overcome the harmful aspects of your upbringing you needed your parents' approval or admission?

This is the key: you don't need them for the second round. It's not up to them to correct what they unwittingly messed up in the first round. It's up to you. It's up to me. It's up to the adult in us.

We need to take responsibility to improve ourselves once we reach the point of awareness about our "childhood baggage".

In my case, the unconditional parental support and permissiveness created a false sense of confidence built upon me having the last word all the time. Or the last bite of a delicious meal. Or everything to what I could attach the words "me first".

It hit me hard when I went to school and people started saying no to me, when my ideas were not the best, when I had to argue logically to back up what I said or wanted, when I saw that there are other opinions out there, too. You'd think that I had slowly started to open up to the opinions of others as time passed.

Oh, no. Not me.

I argued, sulked, belittled, pretended I didn't care, and faked superiority among other things. Needless to say, these behaviors didn't make me the classmate of the year.

Whenever I felt the slightest shake in my sense of self—*Am I doing things right? Am I really that special, important, or correct?*—my parents were at my back, readily confirming that yes, indeed, I was right, and special, and the other kids were just jealous of me for being so special. I didn't need more reassurance after that, and I had no more doubts. I added a new prompt to my obnoxiousness library: "You're just jealous of me."

When I was about fourteen to fifteen years old, I moved to Hungary from Romania to start high school. In my teenage years the behaviors I had learned at home stayed with me and repeatedly surfaced. Many times I hit the social version of rock bottom, and I didn't have my parents nearby to support me. Maybe that was for the best.

The more of an outcast I became, the more my insecurities grew and the more I lost that fake sense of confidence that kept my head high as a child. I simply didn't understand what was happening, why I was so wrong, or why I didn't make any real friends. I was spoiled, lacked empathy and self-awareness, and felt entitled to superior treatment—but at the same time I loved people and desperately wanted to be loved back.

The problem was, I didn't understand what loving someone really meant in action. All I could give was what my parents taught me: encouraging words, flattery, and verbal support for no real reason. The people who really needed such reassurance, again, followed me for a while and enjoyed my company. But once they had enough verbal boosting or just simply had enough of my self-centrism, they left me.

Over the years I didn't get much clarity over what was wrong with me. Why were such things repeatedly happening to me? How could I stop this cycle?

In fact, I was convinced I couldn't stop it. I thought I was normal, and fine, and had nothing to improve on. Other people were at fault for not accepting me. I accepted them, so I thought; therefore, they were the bad guys for not doing the same for me. I cultivated a lot of anxiety and anger towards others, and the more people turned their backs on me, the greater my fear of abandonment grew.

This fear translated extremely poorly to my romantic relationships; I was anxiously attached, neurotically clingy, wildly codependent, and a displeased people pleaser. I had no boundaries. Even when someone hurt me, I withdrew to compliance just to avoid being abandoned. But at the same time my overinflated, childish ego was revolting, so in many cases I snapped and became defensive. My relationships became this toxic cycle of defensiveness, fear of abandonment, withdrawal, sense of oppression—repeat.

I can see these patterns clearly today, but if you asked me two years ago I would have been extremely upset with you. *How dare you call me clingy, egotistical? Mind your own darn business.* I think I'm being too generous with the two-year figure. Even last year I had serious blind spots about my shortcomings.

But I'm lucky that I discovered how my childhood baggage still, almost thirty years later, affects my life and sabotages my happiness. I put in the hard work, the hours of journaling, lots of work in therapy, books, and conversations with people who are more ahead of me on this journey to change for the better. No one could have done this work for me. No one could have convinced me to start doing this work until I was ready.

The more I understand my own path the more I can see the same or similar traits in other people. Today I know how liberating it can be to understand these traits and to work towards actively undoing them. My greatest hope, or current life mission, is to help everyone deal with their own traumas, and get their life on the track their true, adult self wants to be so they can live as freely and happily as possible.

The lessons I want to provide with my story are the following:

- Externally boosted confidence is fragile and collapses quickly once the sources stop fueling it;

- When the same patterns keep repeating in your life, become suspicious of your own behavior. Ask yourself: "What do I do that makes people treat me a certain way?" Ask others: "How do I make you feel? Why?" And then listen to feedback;

- Unexamined and unchanged bad childhood habits will keep your emotional maturity on a child's level, even if you're physically forty;

- Unexamined and unchanged bad childhood habits will fester over time. The older you get, the more harmful these childish habits will become. The behavior the world forgives from a four-year-old won't be forgiven from a forty-four-year-old;

- Don't hold grudges against your parents for their mistakes in your upbringing. It's too late for them to change either themselves or you. You need to take charge of your own improvement once you know what you want to change. Liberate your spirit from bitterness;

- True confidence comes from accepting and embracing our shortcomings, not masking them;

- Correcting a painting is easier when it is in the light, not in the dark. Self-correction is the same. Bring your true nature into the light;

- The adult you should rely on for sustaining self-improvement is yourself. No one else will be as permanently close to you as yourself. Parents, partners, friends can all drift away—or pass away—but you're stuck with yourself to your last day; and

- Knowledge will make you less anxious. Even if you repeat your past mistakes occasionally, it makes all the difference in the world to know where these patterns are coming from. You'll know that you're not a crazy, hopeless, or bad person. You're wounded, you carry scars, and the reactions you give today, at some point in your life, made sense and maybe even kept you alive. This way you'll be more compassionate with yourself, and by accepting more of your dark side you'll actually heal better.

Self-knowledge and self-understanding are powerful tools. Without them confidence can't be genuine, as whatever you're placing your confidence in might not be real. And you can feel it. When you act confidently in a setting you don't know you're good at or you know you're not skilled in, your confidence will come off as fake, exaggerated, or awkward.

Confident people are secure in their worth, and they can only be secure if they know their worth. Self-worth includes the good, the bad, and the ugly, and still shines within. True self-worth needs self-knowledge.

How do you gain self-knowledge?

Through vulnerability: Going out there, trying, failing or succeeding, learning, and trying again.

Through self-reflection: Asking questions about yourself and answering them, journaling, following your emotions, and assessing their true origin.

Confidence is not innate and is not universal. Feeling confident once won't grant you never-ending confidence. You need to show up for yourself day by day, with a mindset that you are enough, you are good, and you can do it. If you can be there for yourself, life will be a less scary, dangerous journey. The more times you can prove that you are there for yourself, and you're able to handle a situation, the more naturally confidence will come to you.

In this book, I'll help you discover your main childhood scars, wounds, and their consequences in your adult life. Then, by accepting them, the book will help you build the kind of confidence in yourself that will stick with you in the long run. I will present chapter by chapter the life areas that are weakened if you don't know or trust yourself, and share with you proven practices that can strengthen your confidence. These practices will help you establish a habitual belief of being good enough. Say yes to opportunities, get the chance to prove your competence for yourself, and gain more and more confidence.

Lack of self-confidence can spring from many things including childhood traumas, early adulthood struggles, workplace-related insecurities, and so on. If you have had enough of being afraid, feeling isolated, and having sweaty palms, the time has come to change that.

I will help you. I will be your crutch. But don't forget, you will have to learn how to walk. You already are much more ahead of yourself than you were ten minutes ago. You made the decision: You got this book. You are already on the road to being the leading lady or man of your new story. Embrace it.

Chapter 2 – Old vs. New Identity

"The rear-view mirror is small for a reason. It is for a reference, not your destination." - Unknown

Whatever you experience in your childhood, you build a series of reactions around it. If you experienced some kind of trauma in your early years, your psyche will develop a mental barrier to protect you from further harm. Your brain will try to minimize the effect of the trauma on you.

If as a kid you've been constantly yelled at for asking questions, you'll learn that asking questions is dangerous—so you'll stop improving your skill of asking questions. Later in life when someone asks you a question you may become agitated or anxious, encounter your mental block, and react to that question either with withdrawal (your fearful childhood self) or with defensiveness and dismissiveness (the way you learned one should react to questions from your parents).

But in your adulthood no one will care if this behavior is something you developed during childhood and you simply never learned to do better. People will just judge you for being a snappy, unpleasant fellow who can't answer a simple question and is impossible to talk to. From their perspective, they are right. From your perspective, you're just doing what you learned before. If you're honest with yourself, you'll see that these learned protective mechanisms don't serve you anymore.

You can change these mechanisms.

Anything horrible, upsetting, or fear-triggering that happened to you is a trauma. But your reactions to it are not who you are. You can change your old, habitual trauma responses—you can recover and be who you truly want to be.

If you choose to find purpose in your pain, trauma won't define you anymore. You can recondition yourself. You can overcome your past hurts; not by denying them, but by seeking wisdom in them and moving forward. Learn to live well. Your negative childhood patterns are part of your life's story, but they are not your life's purpose.

Get Clarity on Your Childhood Traumas

Constantly ruminating about your traumas may feel like thinking and processing them on the surface, but in reality, repeatedly talking or thinking about, reacting over, or denying the same grievances will just magnify your symptoms. Without any new understanding and input towards a solution, you'll just chew the same bone over and over. The more you chew on it, the worse it will taste.

First you need to change your thoughts about your childhood or later traumas. Then you need to learn new responses. Once you're able to do that, you can link new visions and wishes to how you want to deal with these issues in the future.

Before we move on, please take a moment to sit down and identify your greatest traumas and bad childhood behaviors—whatever you have from your past that hinders you today.

1.

2.

3.

When you are done listing your traumas, try to identify the emotions their recalling triggered in you. Did you have any flashbacks, discomfort, tension, sadness, or fear? Write down the feelings you felt next to each trauma. Be mindful of this process: If it is too overwhelming, try to discuss this topic with a therapist.

1.

2.

3.

The longer you live with traumas or life-altering events from your youth, the more bitterly you may feel about how much these problems affected your life. Name a few occasions when your unprocessed traumas prevented you from living your life to the fullest.

1.

2.
3.

How would you like to feel instead?

1.

2.

3.

Please take your time in answering these questions. This is a form of cognitive behavioral therapy where you consciously redirect your old, negative neural pathways and lead your thoughts toward your true, positive wishes. Believe it or not, this is a huge step. By facing your traumas, identifying your emotions related to them, quantifying their negative real-life impact, and naming your authentic desires, you took ownership over your life. You know your emotions now—and you also see where those emotions lead you. You can see the discrepancy between where you are now and where you want to be. You also know the obstacles that stand in your way to get to your desired place.

It's in your hands what you do with this discovery. It's up to you to change. No one can take your desires away from you anymore; no one can sabotage or negatively influence you. You are the leader of your life. You can have clarity, peace, and joy.

Don't be afraid to change your old habits learned from past traumas. You have nothing to lose, but a lot to gain. Your emotions are conditioned reactivity, not reality. They don't have to control your life. Identify your biggest fears: The things that keep you from living your best life.

1.

2.

3.

When you are done, check your first list where you identified your traumas and see how many of your fears are legitimate and how many are a result of trauma conditioning. Your fears are not a bad thing. They are quite useful right now. Thanks to them, you can gain absolute clarity on what your darkest subconscious conditioned beliefs are and, therefore, you'll know from where you should start seeking the light.

What we need in enlightening moments like this is empowerment. It's scary to recognize and name your biggest traumas.

It's liberating and hard at the same time to accept that the solution to live a better life was within me all along. All these years I suffered from the consequences of my traumas I could have written a different story. It was my responsibility to change my traumas even though they were not my fault. This realization is powerful.

What methods did you use in the past to control and gain power over your traumas? Anger? Stonewalling? Defensiveness? Write them down.

Did any of them work? Why? Which were not helpful? Why?

1.

2.

3.

These coping mechanisms mostly align themselves to negativity, am I right? Time to let some sunshine in.

Start by no longer identifying yourself as a survivor. You read that correctly. Survivorship, as mighty and positive as it sounds, still binds you to your trauma and keeps you adhered to a trauma-related identity. Why are you a survivor? Because you *survived* a trauma.

Identifying with survivorship may create a sense of obligation in you to remain defined by your trauma, otherwise you lose your identity. You are a person with a growth mindset. No need for other explanatory, fancy labels.

Take some time and think about what you would like to ditch from your life.

1.

2.

3.

Now create a list of the things you want to have and experience.

1.

2.

3.

Empower your mind with good intentions toward yourself, focus on what you want, and distance yourself from the trauma. Process your fears from a safe place in an introspective way. You are slowly rewiring your brain by approaching your past from a different angle. Your thoughts affect your neural pathways. Send healing, changing messages to your brain to get rid of your negative self-sabotaging thoughts for good.

In this chapter we unveiled your greatest traumas, the things that hold you back from living your best life. If you didn't complete the exercises, go back and fill in the blanks with your thoughts. It's important to gain awareness about the real reasons that keep you in an emotional rut. Explore, embrace, and then learn to respond differently.

How? The next chapters will help you.

Chapter 3 – Progress

I'm aware of my issues and I love myself. I will do my best to change them to improve my life.

Change is the key to solving any problem you recognize in yourself. Do you think you can't change? Or maybe you tried, but stopped halfway because you occasionally relapsed? Don't give up on yourself. Change doesn't happen overnight and it won't be perfect.

How do you approach change that enhances confidence in general?

1. **Find your whys**. In other words, ask yourself: Why do I feel I can't change? Why do I prefer not to

do it? For what purpose do I seek change? What beliefs are holding me back?

2. **Become assertive**. Select a few areas in your life where you'd like to be more assertive. Becoming assertive and protecting your boundaries empowers you. It helps you become more grounded.

By selecting a few areas where you start drawing a line that other people are not allowed to cross, you'll gain some control over your life. Be very specific when you determine in which area and how exactly you want to practice assertiveness. For example, "I want to be assertive at my workplace." is a very vague definition. You arrive at your workplace and then what? Right?

But if you instead make a plan like "I will protect my boundaries with my colleague who regularly unloads a part of their work onto me by saying 'I'm sorry but

I don't have the capacity to do this.'" it sounds a bit more different, right? Start with easier situations so you can successfully complete them and get some momentum in building confidence for the more challenging scenarios.

3. **Take responsibility**. If you want to retrain your brain, seek to understand what your responsibility is in getting to the point in your life where you are now. Traumatic childhood experiences are not your fault. But your current reaction to them is your responsibility. Taking ownership of your life starts with "I am responsible. I want to do that, and it's up to me to do it."

As much as your traumas are legitimate reasons for you to be pissed and bitter, if you hide behind a protective wall of placing blame, you might boost your sense of justice but you won't change the fact that you spend your life behind that wall. You know your traumas now and you know how they affect you. It's your responsibility to take action to change them. Do it for yourself.

4. Learn to let go. Allow yourself to let go of your past. Learn your lessons, draw your conclusions, and then escape the grip of it. It's hard when you were victimized, I know that. Being victimized kicks you off balance. You get detached from your true self—you're confused. As a child you have two options to believe when something traumatic happens to you:

1. My parent is bad for hurting me this way and doing this to me.
2. I am bad, and that's why this happened to me.

As you can imagine, our fragile childhood psyche can't handle option 1. If you accepted as a kid that your parent is the one at fault, you'd fundamentally shake your sense of security. If the parent is bad, it means that he or she is not capable of taking care of you, of granting you safety. No safety equals no life in a child's mind.

Option 2, therefore, is a safer choice. You are bad. And the road to safety leads through not triggering the parent with the action that put you at risk.

In my case, it was withdrawing from asking questions and wondering about the whys behind someone's actions. The more I learned to not ask questions, the more numb and detached I felt from others. But in reality I detached from myself. I was in full survival mode; my father's behavior was frightening and shocking. I disassociated from my genuine curiosity.

Dissociation is a smart coping skill the brain develops to deal with the confusion that those who were supposed to care for us were the same people who hurt us. The safest way is to empathize with your wrongdoer for the sake of safety. But empathizing with the wrongdoer will leave no room for empathy for yourself. No one will be on your side, therefore you'll believe that you are wrong and worthless. If you were right, someone would be on your team, right? You trade your sense of self-worth in order to survive.

We tend to do this deep into our adulthood when we have unresolved issues from our past. This way, the senseless suffering makes more sense—it is more tolerable, less painful. Year by year this feeling of worthlessness and invisibility stacks in layers, keeping you from truly trusting that anyone could care about you. Numbing yourself as a way of coping drastically decreases self-awareness and belonging.

Do you ever feel detached or numb from past or present experiences? Write down a few examples. Do you notice any resemblance between past and present detachment or numbing? If so, try to define some repeating patterns.

1.

2.

3.

You just recognized some very important past–present connections. From now on you can consciously work with these.

Detachment and numbing are natural responses to secure survival when facing immediate trauma. By staying calm in a crisis, your chances of surviving grow. The trick is to stop being detached right after the "danger" is gone, otherwise you'll feel like a lobotomized zombie throughout your life. You may seem okay on the surface, but you are out of touch with your emotions. You're reactive instead of intentional. You may do something and then be totally confused: "Why did I even do that?" or "I don't know what has gotten into me. I just acted on an impulse."

These impulses are the parts of us that are repressed by detachment, but desperately want to surface. The fact that we don't understand these repressed emotions makes us reactive, out of control, and sometimes even the "bad guy".

For example, I often snapped at my partner when he triggered something from my childhood. I didn't understand why I reacted with hostility to him. My reaction made him feel unloved and hurt without a real reason. From his perspective, it didn't matter why I behaved the way I did. He just knew he didn't deserve that treatment—rightfully so. He didn't deserve it. I unleashed my daddy issues on him. And that's not fair, not right, and it didn't improve my life—much less his.

It is essential to get back in touch with our emotions and feelings, not only for our own sakes but for the sake of others. I think we have the moral obligation to heal our wounds and not bleed on others. I learned this the hard way.

Constant rumination and distress about your actions or about the deeds of your wrongdoers are not the state of mind you want to live in. We all need to learn to reconnect with our emotions, stop cultivating anger against our perpetrators, and turn our focus toward a better future. To do this, first we need to find the things that keep us detached and numb.

Which fears or thoughts have such power over you that they paralyze you from being connected to yourself or others?

1.

2.

3.

Detachment and dissociation are defense mechanisms which generate an internal struggle with the outside world. You may be able to keep your struggles inside for the time being when you interact with others, but inside you'll still feel confused, blocked, and afraid, all with an inability to trust. When you feel too overwhelmed by your internal stress, you snap and react in a harmful way to people who are not the cause of your suffering. You not only hurt them but also yourself by doing so.

People won't understand why you snapped; they will become self-protective and distant. Their reaction will reinforce in you that you are unlovable, that you will be abandoned, and that you are not worthy. It is a vicious cycle.

You need to break the mental chains that bind you and learn to get in touch with your feelings before they erupt in destructive ways. Understand your behavioral patterns and catch them before they escalate.

Here is an exercise you can do when you feel emotionally overwhelmed to ground yourself and prevent a potential snap.

1. Sit down comfortably.

2. Take three deep, soothing breaths. Inhale through your nose and exhale through your mouth. Close your eyes.

3. Gently put your palms over your eyes. Stay like that for a few seconds while breathing naturally. Then slowly move your fingertips onto your temples and apply soft pressure in a circular motion. This will stimulate your amygdala, which is responsible for the fight-or-fight response. Relax.

4. Move your fingertips all the way down your jawline, and then drag your fingers back until you reach your vertebrae on your spine.

5. Rest your palms here and take another deep breath.

6. Then with an even lighter pressure, pull your fingertips under your jaw. Release all tension here, and then move your hands slowly to your throat.

Cover your throat protectively with your hands as if you'd want to choke yourself—but be very gentle, just give yourself a soft, protective feeling. The throat is where your vagus nerve descends. Make it feel protected. Then slowly release your hands in your lap.

7. Relax and take a couple normal breaths. Feel the changes this exercise created in your body. Try to recognize every sensation: Tingling, pulsing, itching, relaxing sensations. You are alive, you are here and now.

8. Shift your focus onto your feet. Touch the ground with them intentionally, in case they are not touching it already. Then slowly stand up, gluing your focus to your feet. Stand up, feel that you are grounded.

Practice this short exercise multiple times daily and notice the calming benefits it provides. When you find yourself in a stressful situation, feeling anxiety, or being triggered, quickly massage through your temple, jawline, back of the neck, and neck before reacting. Shift your focus for a second onto your feet. Feel the soothing ground under it. You are safe. You are not a victim. You have the power to react differently. Be calm, be present.

Chapter 4 – Break Free from Dishonesty

When you are a kid, your identity is fragile and your need to feel safe surpasses almost any other wish. The key to survival is parental love, attention, and care. When you do something that your parent deems bad and withholds love from you, your subconscious mind stores that event as something you should beware repeating. For example, if you asked questions that made your parent angry, you'll learn to systematically edit yourself before speaking to ensure that you won't get into trouble. You will learn to pay attention to the triggers of different people (especially those who are important to you) and you'll start acting in a way to avoid triggering them. But while on the surface you may avoid conflict and be liked, deep down you're lying to yourself and others.

Generally the areas we felt most unresolved as children will be the areas most prone to dishonesty. In these areas we'll be less likely to admit that what we learned in our youth influenced who we became, and still affects our lives as adults. The more unsatisfied we are with our current life, the harder it is to rip off the bandage of unhelpful behavior learned in childhood. The more skewed our self-image is and the more we lie about who we are, the more we'll blame others for our problems instead of taking responsibility for our part.

Let me tell you a personal story to illustrate my point.

I struggle with a huge, traumatic fear of abandonment. When I was two years old, my mom went back to work to a different town, so I was growing up at my grandparents and seeing my parents only on the weekends. The weekly, heartbreaking goodbyes turned me into a very anxious child. Then, at the age of seven when I moved in together with my parents, I missed my grandparents dearly—who by that point had become the main adult figures in my life.

One year later I "lost" my mother to schizophrenia.

Seven years later I lost both of my grandparents for good.
Then one year later I "lost" my father when he betrayed my trust, stealing the heritage I got from my grandparents, investing the money poorly. He lost it, and without even an apology, left me as a beggar in a foreign country.

Loss, loss, abandonment.

I used to be very bitter about my story before. All I focused on were questions like "Why me?" and "What if?" and "How could you?" and then back to "Why me?" all over again. Today I know that there was no reason. My childhood experiences were not happening purposefully to ruin my life. Even my dad stripping me of my heritage that would have assured me an easier life in a foreign land was not an action meant to cause me harm directly. My dad, the gullible, naive narcissist, wanted to get rich fast, whatever the cost. He was falling for Ponzi schemes as others fall for Game of Thrones. If something had a peak, he jumped on it.

These traumatic events didn't leave me without scars. In my romantic relationships I became very anxiously attached. I always felt insecure, unsafe in my relationships, yet I was convinced that it was the man's job to make me feel safe. It never occurred to me that if I felt unsafe, that it had something to do with me. Nope. The guy wasn't showing enough commitment, wasn't caring enough, and didn't give me enough words of affirmation.

I moved the goal post constantly. Whenever a guy learned to text me more often, I wanted something else as "proof". If only he'd tell me "I love you." more often, introduce me to more friends, would propose to me, then I would feel safe. These unreasonable expectations showed themselves in my behavior. I blamed him for my emotions: "You're the reason why I feel so insecure." This often left the men in my life feeling unappreciated, belittled, falsely accused, and unloved. I never felt safe despite their efforts.

I was dishonest in my earlier relationships as I couldn't admit the truth that the only reason I felt unsafe was because I learned in my youth that people will always leave me. It had nothing to do with my current partner. I also learned to do anything to keep them in my life because my subconscious told me that I couldn't survive without them. In my childhood, this belief might have been true, but not in my adulthood. Ultimately, I had to see that the men in my life could do nothing to make me feel truly safe. It was a childhood trauma I had to face and overcome.

I understand today how much pain my unresolved childhood problems caused for many well-meaning men and myself. This was all rooted in my inability to be honest with myself.

Did you ever do anything similar? Name three things you know you were dishonest about.

1.

2.

3.

Why? Do you know the underlying cause of your dishonesty?

1.

2.

3.

Self-deception is bleeding from many wounds. It doesn't help your self-esteem and neither will it help your social relationships. People will be affected negatively. We can vegetate in dishonesty for years. But the solution is in our pocket.

Let me explain it with Plato's famous allegory of the cave.

The story begins with people sitting in a cave around a fire; the only world they know is inside the cave. Let's say you start feeling that the fire is too hot, that something's wrong by just sitting around this burning fire all the time. What if you experimented? How does it feel to distance yourself from the fire? Frightening to step out, isn't it? But once you're outside, you see splendid green fields and feel the sun comfortably warming your skin. Because you've been in that cave all your life, your eyes are weak and can't adjust to the bright daylight, so you have to squint. Everything around you is beautiful, but it hurts like hell to see it. It made sense to sit next to the fire in the cold cave because you wanted to feel warm. You didn't know there was a sun which gave you the perfect warmth, so you created artificial warmth to keep yourself comfortable. But it was never truly comfortable, was it? And now you know why.

Here you have two options.

You can choose to stay outside, knowing the sun will keep you warm but you'll need to learn to live in this bigger, brighter world. That's effort, and frightening. Or, you can choose to go back into the cave where it is dark, and while the fire may be too hot, you're feeling comfortable and secure. Of course, it won't be the same now. Now you've seen the world outside. When you're sitting there in the cave, you will know there is more to life than what you're experiencing.

Change begins at the moment when you become aware of your unhealthy behavior, and start to feel uncomfortable because of it.

If you bought this book, it means you are already aware of some issues you have. Your big moment of realization could have been provoked by anything—

an inspiring person, a big failure, losing someone close to you, or just like in my case, a book.

It doesn't matter. It also doesn't matter how many years you've lived without this knowledge. Those years have passed now, and getting stuck in mourning them won't make your life better. Filling your head with thoughts like "If I knew this *X* years ago, then..." won't move you in a better direction. Deciding to not change is also not a great option. It's not too late for you to change. If it takes one year, two years, to unlearn lifelong habits, so what? Those two years will pass anyway. Why not fill your days with thoughts and actions that serve a better future?

Change is never easy. You had an identity and now new information and new types of identity-shaping forces are attacking your psyche. Your current habits run deep under your skin. You're going to have to scrub away at it, and just like seeing the sun for the first time, it is going to be painful. There's always pain in change. It's a kind of death experience. The stages of grief apply also when you are releasing an old part of your personality.

Many people make a mistake. They think if they just take a shower and maybe exfoliate a bit, go to a little therapy, read a book, jot down some affirmations, their job is done. Nope. That's just the surface solution that will make you feel better in the short term, but to really build a lasting and solid foundation will take more than that.

First and foremost, it will take time. You will relapse occasionally. Therefore you have to get very familiar with the lies you tell yourself. Don't beat yourself up too harshly over it, all of us are affected by self-deception and dishonesty. Some more than others.

Remember, our lies reflect what we wish were true. When you were dishonest about something, what was the real wish behind it? (Use the answers you gave previously.)

1.

2.

3.

The problem in most cases is that we can't handle reality, the truth. We don't have the mental strength to face the world as it is. We fabricate some lies instead to make us feel better, safer. We also create lies because we hate to deal with the consequences of the truth. We don't want to see our ugly parts, our damaged self. We don't want to acknowledge the harm others caused us and what we became by how we responded to these harmful circumstances.

When we accept the truth, we are forced to take a hard look at ourselves and see the parts we don't want to admit to having. In this sense, dishonesty and lies are a good survival strategy because they give immediate relief of the most painful part of human life.

Sigmund Freud described the many ways we lie to ourselves through ego defense mechanisms. He suggested that humans use a broad spectrum of psychological strategies to protect ourselves from any information that would cause pain to our ego. Let's talk about the most common ego defense mechanisms.

Denial

When we are in denial, we are lying to ourselves that something is true even though it isn't (or vice versa).

For example, someone is convinced that Ponzi schemes can make them rich quickly. They constantly fail to achieve the desired success yet also fail to admit that their beliefs might have set prematurely on this type of moneymaking. There is always an excuse why the Ponzi scheme isn't working: There are no quality people on our team, or the economy is in a downward spiral. Denial can sometimes be so powerful that we even blame ourselves instead of reevaluating our beliefs, such as noting that the tip of the Ponzi pyramid has a Ferrari. *The problem must be with me*, the person thinks, because they can't make enough money through this business to buy a Ferrari themselves. There isn't a problem with the business structure itself.

The more people try to tell us the truth about what we're denying, the more vehemently we will stick to our guns.

Name the biggest denials you can identify in your life.

1.

2.

3.

Rationalization

We rationalize when we lie to ourselves by creating a reason to excuse our behavior.

I wouldn't have withheld affection from you if you didn't snap at me—justifying lack of affection. I'm not going to tolerate any undereducated boss yelling at me—justifying unemployment. I know that drinking is bad for me but it helps me relax after a long day at work—making someone feel better about an unhealthy habit.

List some rationalizations you can identify in your life.

1.

2.

3.

Regression

When we act more immaturely than would be expected of our age, we do regression.

For example, when instead of holding a responsible, adult disagreement, you're throwing a five-year-old's temper tantrum. When someone wanted to talk his issues through with his partner, this is the conversation they had:

> **Husband:** It really hurts me when you dismiss my side like that. I don't feel you're taking responsibility for your actions.
>
> **Wife:** I always take responsibility. Always.
>
> **Husband:** But by not admitting that you took away that money and denying how much harm you've caused me, you're not taking responsibility.
>
> **Wife:** Yes, I am. If you don't like what I say, stop asking. These are the facts.
>
> **Husband:** You're not listening to me.
>
> **Wife:** Yes I am.
>
> **Husband:** Okay. Then can you repeat what I said?
>
> **Wife:** I don't need to prove anything. (Sulking.)

Husband: You're making this conversation quite difficult.

Wife: Then I'm difficult. I don't care.

It was impossible to break through the wife's walls of defenses. At the end of this conversation she sat with arms and legs crossed on the chair, rolling her eyes and mocking his tone. There was no one to have an adult discussion with.

In what situations do you use regression? Why?

1.

2.

3.

Projection

When we use projection, we take a disliked quality of ourselves and attribute it to someone else.

For example, when we feel attracted to someone at our workplace, we start nagging our partner about how much they love us, if they plan to leave us, and so on. Or when you fear opening up about your most painful memories, you accuse your friends of not being totally honest with you.

This type of projection is called negative projection. There is a flipside of projection, however: Positive projection, which can be just as harmful. For example, you work hard on changing yourself for the better and therefore you assume that your partner will also do the same. So you start having expectations of your partner that could only be realistic if they indeed started to change. But just because you have a positive quality doesn't mean the other person has it as well.

What traits can you identify that you project onto other people?

1.

2.

3.

Displacement

When we use this ego defense mechanism, we take our anger or displeasure out on people or objects that are less threatening than what or who made us angry.

In other words, we take our negative emotions out on someone or something that is less frightening or dangerous. For example, instead of lashing out at your boss who humiliated you in front of your colleagues, you yell at your husband who forgot to feed the dog. Or instead of telling your overly critical mother that she stepped out of line, you smash a dozen eggs on the wall.

Recall some occasions when you used displacement as a way of calming down.

1.

2.

3.

Which of these ego defense mechanisms do you use most often? Do you experience similar events? These somewhat innocent, but still seriously harmful, altered realities keep you from taking responsibility and becoming your true self.

"We deceive ourselves because we don't have enough psychological strength to admit the truth and deal with the consequences that will follow," says Cortney S. Warren, Ph.D.

Self-deception can leave you with tremendous regret and shame. Looking back at a period full of retrospective regret is a bitter pill to swallow—especially if the self-deceptive period lasted a long time. You cannot change that past, but you can have more clarity in the future. If you want to learn how to leave self-deception behind and be true to yourself, try out these steps.

1. Identify your true values.

Sit down somewhere where you can be alone, undisturbed, and truly honest with yourself. What do you care the most about in this world? Are you acting in accordance with them? Specify what you want to achieve, who you want to be, and then set smaller goals to get there. Small goals, with the promise of a big one, can give you purpose and power.

My main values are:

1.

2.

3.

2. Practice mindfulness.

Oh, that negative, evil little voice in your head! If only it could shut up a little... It can. Listen to your thoughts during random moments of the day. Make a mental note about recurring negative thoughts and sit down to check their validity. Are they really true?

For example: "I could never act spontaneously. That's not who I am." If you are convinced of this, think about why you are so sure about this self-limiting belief. When did you decide who you can and can't be? How many years ago did you cast a verdict on yourself about what you could and couldn't do? Why? Be honest with yourself. Don't underestimate yourself.

"Human beings will absolutely follow through on who they believe they are." - Tony Robbins

Everybody acts consistent with who they believe they are. The strongest force in the human personality is the need to stay consistent with how people define themselves. If you define yourself as someone who isn't spontaneous, you won't act crazily, unpredictably, or surprisingly. That's not who you are, after all. Most people set themselves life standards ten, twenty, or more years ago—maybe in their childhood as a defense mechanism. But they consider these standards "who they really are" just because they can't remember or imagine how to be different. This is deceptive self-conditioning.

Our thoughts are related to our feelings and behavior. We tend to think in outdated or illogical ways. This leads us to outdated, irrationality-based emotions and actions. If we can change our thought patterns to be more consistent with reality, our emotions and behaviors will also be more logical and realistic. For example, if you keep repeating to yourself, "I'm incapable of spontaneity and I so hate people who keep on nagging me to engage in such activities," you will probably feel some self-righteous anger and snap at your friends.

If you can shift your thinking to be more reasonable, your reaction will also change. For example, "I didn't do spontaneous things for a long time, so I'm not sure how I will feel about it. My friends will be there so things can't turn to be that bad, but I feel so uncomfortable because being spontaneous is totally out of my comfort zone." You still won't feel great about being thrown into the deep water of spontaneity, but you'll see reality as it is. Spontaneity is something you didn't do for a long time. This is an objectively correct statement. You being incapable of being spontaneous isn't. Your friends pushing you out of your comfort zone is an honest realization, you hating your friends isn't.

Our reactions reflect who we are. We are responsible for our reactions even if what generated our pain was objectively terrible and not our fault. Victor Frankl, the father of logotherapy and a survivor of the Auschwitz concentration camps, said: "The one thing you can't take away from me is the way I choose to respond to what you do to me."

We don't really think about this, but there are people out there who are now trying to heal from what we did to them just as we are trying to heal from what they did to us. The ways in which we lie to ourselves will not only hurt us, but we can cause a great deal of psychological distress to those around us.

When we choose not to change despite our realizations that we should, we need to take full responsibility of this choice and its consequences. It's our choice to act outside of our best interest despite acknowledging the truth. Not changing is also a choice and we need to embrace the following statement:

"I don't feel good about myself. Now I know the reason why and I know what I should do to feel better, yet I'm not willing to do it. However, I also pledge not to speak negatively about my life anymore. I will accept what is true, but embrace the life that I have and try to be as fulfilled as possible with my life as it is."

When you are honest with yourself but you don't change, that's your choice. If change seems like the worse option, try your best to be happy with what you have and who you are today.

But don't forget that each moment is perfect to change your stance. You can choose to change at any moment. If you voted to not change a day ago, you have the right to rewrite that stance today. You can start changing any moment. You can start to change right now.

Chapter 5 – Acknowledgement and Acceptance

Acknowledge your qualities and your flaws. What do you think? How do you feel about yourself? Objectively look inside yourself. People speak about qualities like consciousness, self-knowledge, and confidence as if these concepts were obvious and clear, but in fact they are not quite sure what these things really mean.

Consciousness will take shape only if you start thinking about your qualities. It's a kind of metacognition, thinking about your thoughts, and assessing your feelings about your feelings.

If your flaws upset you, don't hide them, don't sweep them under the carpet. Don't be dishonest.

That won't help you, as we saw in the previous chapter. Rather, begin to embrace them and speak about them. When you do this, self-deception will disappear. Only the truth will remain.

And the truth will hurt.

Let's say you were blindfolded for ten or fifteen years. If after many years you choose to remove the blinders, when you open your eyes even the slightest bit, it will hurt. So first you have to acknowledge that opening your eyes will be painful.

Most of the people who get this far usually quit because they can't endure the pain, and they fear failure. What if they stick to all the pain change requires and, in the end, their life still won't be better? So they decide to do nothing, and they stick their heads back in the sand.

What happens if you decide to see? After the pain (or shall I say, during) you will start to recall one by one all the chances you missed, all the possibilities you didn't take, all the people you hurt, and all the time you wasted. It is important to take a hard look at these events and harness their lessons. Try not to ruminate about the wasted past; rather, just make some mental notes about what you want to do differently in the future. Stay in the present.

The greatest lessons I can extract from my pain are:

1.

2.

3.

Accept that pain is necessary for development. Understand that not only does happiness makes you feel alive, so does pain. Everything you experience today had its cause in the past. Your task today is only to learn from them. But without these causes you wouldn't be who you are today. Everything has its purpose in this life, the same as the light and the darkness.

Prepare yourself for some further challenges. You, who are starting to live honestly, will now see that the people around you are not as honest as you thought they were. You will see their blindness and how they mismanage their lives. Refrain from judgment, don't educate them or tell them how "dumb" (or wrong or blind) they are for not seeing what you see. On one hand they didn't ask for your opinion, on the other hand they need to see reality for themselves when they are ready. You know better than anyone, you can't open your eyes until you're truly ready. This readiness has to come from within.

The best you can do is to lead people with a good example. Only if your new way of living triggers some curiosity in them and they ask for your help should you tell them your "truth". Honesty is a dangerous weapon and you should be cautious when you use it. If you are too frank, too direct, you might kick them into defensiveness. It is better to ask the right questions and let your friends answer them. You know, just as there are "white lies" there is also "white honesty".

When you start seeing clearly and the painful period softens, you will breathe much easier. You will be filled with energy; you will have the will to go further on your way to self-discovery. You will start to realize your true virtues and flaws and how much easier and rewarding life can be if you live by them. Don't be scared of them. Accept them. Everything you are now is the result of your past actions, and all you will be in the future will be the result of what you are doing now.

The best thing you can do now is picture what kind of a person you would like to be in the future. Write it down; write at least ten aspects of your desired self. What qualities would you like to have, which of your current behaviors would you like to minimize?

1.

2.

3.

4.

5.

6.

7.

8.

9.

10.

There are certain things in life that you can't influence—they are not within your control. These include illnesses, economy changes, and other people's behavior. The only thing you can change in these cases is your attitude: How you choose to think and feel about them. When you decide to change your attitude, you won't look at these events as unjust tragedies that happened to make you miserable, but as events that can add value to your growth, even if you don't understand their meaning right now.

Nothing lasts forever—neither good nor bad. Life is ever-changing. So are your circumstances. There is no emotion or situation that will hurt you or make you happy forever. If you are in a sorrowful phase of your life, take comfort in the power of impermanence. If you're overly joyful, take caution. This doesn't mean that things will be horrible after they are good. It's up to you from what perspective you approach things in life.

You may think now that this all sounds great and I gave you an excellent pep talk, but what are you supposed to do now? What I told you sounds appealing, but you feel extremely helpless in your situation and you don't know how to take action.

I understand that you can be held back by toxic beliefs when you are tangled in a web of wishing for better behaviors. You need a deeper understanding of these things before you can break free of your mental cage.

Let's see how you can transform helplessness to hopefulness.

Traumatic childhood experiences, and a life lived with decreased self-worth, can generate lacking in every area of your life. Becoming hopeful about a better future is necessary to break the chains of the past.

As with everything, first we need to gain awareness about what keeps you hopeless. When do you feel the most helpless?

1.

2.

3.

What or who triggers your helplessness?

1.

2.

3.

Martin Seligman introduced and studied the condition of learned helplessness. It basically comes from conditioning. Imagine a circus elephant which is restrained by putting a rope around its neck and secured to a picket. When the elephant is a baby, the rope is strong enough to keep it still. However, when the elephant grows up, it is still restrained with the same rope. At this point the elephant could easily break free and destroy the entire circus tent if it wishes, but it won't resist or try to escape. Why?

Because the many years of conditioning convinced the elephant that it can't break free from the rope. We act just as this elephant with our early, deep-rooted helplessness conditioning.

The good news is that we can think and therefore change this conditioning. We can also condition ourselves to learn new things like how to be happy, hopeful. and fulfilled.

Before we can do this, however, we need to find the root causes of our current conditioning patterns. Do you keep reliving a helpless or fear-based pattern when you are close to your caregivers, siblings, or other people? Is it trauma related? Money related? Communication related?

Collect everything you may have adopted as a root cause of helplessness in your everyday life.

1.

2.

3.

Acknowledge these discoveries. You didn't come to live on this Earth to live out negative patterns inherited from your family or past experiences. That's not your purpose. Break these patterns by moving closer to your true purpose—whatever you choose that to be. Your past may be part of your story but it doesn't have to be your fate.

Believing you are helpless is a self-chosen trap, but it can feel very real. Feeling helpless, you can truly believe you and your will don't exist—that you are a plastic bag in the world which must obey any wind that blows it, and it's totally out of its control where it'll land. You can be part of the world if you make the conscious choice to ditch the belief of helplessness. Challenge your limiting beliefs. Take a leap of faith and prove to yourself that you can help yourself.

Be self-compassionate. If you try to break out of your helplessness cycle but you fail at first, don't write yourself off. Would you say something like "I knew you couldn't do it." or "You're just a sad loser." to your friend who is struggling with self-improvement? Why would you say that to yourself then? Be compassionate with the lovely person you are, and who is trying so hard to change. By simply succeeding to quiet those harsh inner voices, you'll feel tremendous success. Compassion smashes the roots of helplessness.

What challenges do you have that make you feel helpless? Think about at least one and then fill in for yourself the following anti-helplessness statements.

1. I'm not worthless because
_____
___

2. I'm not helpless because
_____
___

3. I'm hopeful because
_____
_____

Insist on keeping hopefulness in your life in the beginning. Don't fake it 'til you make it. Simply keep the sunray of hope actively present in your mind. Even if it's not easy, even if you feel resistance or anger, try to remember what your hopes are. Ask yourself questions:

Why do I think I can't do this?

What am I hoping for in this situation?

How could I reach what I'm hoping for?

Ask and answer questions from yourself regarding the situation and allow yourself to find a purpose in them.

Note where you feel helplessness in your body. How? Is it an ache, heaviness, numbness?

1.

2.

3.

Now write three hopeful sentences that you can recite when these helpless feelings wash through your body. Be aware of how helplessness feels and, when you notice the sensation, like a Pavlovian dog, start reciting your hopefulness reminders.

1.

2.

3.

Don't worry if your hopeful statements sound unbelievable or too farfetched at the moment. Just listen to what you say, imagine that positivity, and take some deep breaths in and out. Break the cycle of helplessness.

Write down three concrete steps you can do to overcome your habit of helplessness. What can you do to break it in real life? (For example, every time I feel I can't do something I pledge to do something else, smaller, that also seems "unmanageable" to warm up for the big thing.)

1.

2.

3.

Now that you know the manifestations of helplessness in your life, you know how it feels, and you also know what you need to do when these feelings arise. Now it's time to practice your solutions. It will take some time to gain true confidence in yourself, to feel totally cured of helplessness and see yourself as a whole adult.

Hope pushes helplessness away and is a renewable resource. There is always more. Take advantage of it.

Chapter 6 – Guilt and Shame

According to Freud, guilt is generated by the superego to change a person's behavior. Freud's psychoanalytic theory of personality describes the superego as the part of personality made up by one's internalized ideals that they get from parents and society. The superego's task is to repress the urges of the id and get the ego to behave morally, instead of realistically.[i]

Freud, in his theory on psychosexual development, determined the superego to be the last aspect of personality to develop. First the id appears: The basic, primal component of human personality. The id exists from birth. As the child grows and gains awareness, the ego starts to develop. This process happens during the first three years of one's life. The superego starts to get shape around the age of five: Ideas about right and wrong, morals, values learned from the environment, society, and culture all influence the superego.

Freud distinguishes two parts of the superego: The ego ideal and the conscience.

The ego ideal embodies rules and standards for good, approved behaviors. The sense of approval stems from a child's main caregivers and other authority figures. Following these rules gives the person pride: A sense of accomplishment and worth. If the rules are broken, it can result in feelings of guilt. Put plainly, the ego ideal is our ideal self, how we wish to behave on a general basis—what kind of people we'd like to be.

The conscience is responsible for tempering us when we engage in rule breaking—in behaviors that are considered wrong. In other words, when we engage in actions that are against our ego ideal, we feel guilty and ashamed. When we act to conform to our ego ideal, our conscience is clear.

The role of the superego is, on one hand, to repress the socially unacceptable, instinctual urges of the id. On the other hand, the superego tries to guide the ego to act morally. This is not a realistic goal, though. The superego's main purpose is to be morally perfect without considering reality.

The superego invades every level of consciousness. Thus, we can feel guilt occasionally but not understand why. When the superego acts consciously, we understand the resulting feelings. But in the case of the superego acting on the unconscious level, to punish the id, or repress the ego, for instance, we might end up feelings guilt mixed with confusion. We don't really understand why we feel that way.[ii]

Psychologist Dr. Edward S. Kubany defined guilt as a "negative feeling state, which is triggered by the belief that one should have thought, felt, or acted differently."

Where and when did we learn how to feel guilty?

It starts in early childhood. The person you become depends largely on the signals you get from your environment. As a child you crave love, especially when you are young. If your environment gives you the love and encouragement you need, doesn't try to teach you by withholding love, and is consistent in punishments, you will have healthy, secure attachments and self-image later in life.

But if you are harshly judged and often punished inconsistently (one day the "bad" behavior is accepted, the next you face retaliation) you'll become anxious, confused, and your ability to distinguish right from wrong never develops. Your superego will have a hard job, and splashes of unnecessary guilt can invade you in a self-destructive way. And not only guilt, but also something even worse: Shame.

Brené Brown, Ph.D., distinguishes guilt from shame. Guilt is a more constructive emotion, based on her research, as it focuses on behavior. "I did something bad, and I'm feeling guilty." Shame, on the other hand, is an absolutely self-destructive emotion: "I am bad." Guilt, therefore, if kept to a healthy level, can be a useful emotion, driven by a healthy superego, where we accurately distinguish right from wrong. Through guilt we learn to correct socially hurtful behavior. But when guilt is felt inconsistently, and disproportionately, it can be very harmful.

Parents are our primary role models. They should make us feel safe, we crave that. But inconsistent punishments make us feel unsafe and confused. The person who is the source of our greatest safety also becomes the greatest source of fear and pain. Parental anger and the withholding of love results in the loss of safety. What does the child do? He or she tries to avoid situations of punishment to "not lose love again". Therefore they learn people-pleasing as a method to feel safe. But with inconsistent punishments it doesn't matter sometimes how well the child behaves to achieve safety, the parent will still punish them. This is especially true in famIlIes where one of the parents suffers from some kind of addiction or mental illness. At this stage, nothing will feel safe to the child. They will decide that the world is a dangerous, unsafe place, and they should be afraid because hell can break loose anywhere, triggered by anything.

Emotional blackmailing can also generate guilt and shame during punishments.

"You see I do so much for you! I cook for you, I wash your dirty pants, and this is how you repay me? I ask one thing from you, to be home on time and you can't even do that."

Oh, how many times I heard that from my grandmother, may she rest in peace, only because I came home ten minutes later than scheduled. I became anxiously punctual. Even as an adult I am on time or arrive earlier than needed. I'd rather wait. I couldn't bear the guilt of being late. When I am running late because of things outside of my control (like traffic or a slow line) I get overly anxious and stressed. I fear "losing face".

Your adult decision-making process can become guilt driven later in life. When you want to do something—start something new—if it conflicts with the values learned in your childhood, you will hesitate to take action. If you take action, you'll feel guilt for disrespecting your "heritage". If you don't take action, you'll feel guilty for letting yourself down. There's no clear way around it.

If you grow up constantly feeling you are not good enough, even as an adult you'll continue to struggle to fulfill parental or societal expectations.

I was speaking with one of my best friends about guilt and it led us to the topic of feeling guilty about saying no. She told me she often feels guilty when she turns somebody down, even when the person is not close to her, because she feels she let that person down. She will be seen as "not good enough" by that person. People who feel guilty for saying no and prioritizing themselves put the interests of others before their own. They lack a strong sense of self-esteem and have poor boundaries. Thus they risk being taken advantage of frequently.

If you recognize yourself, don't worry. Being able to say no and developing healthy boundaries is learnable. You don't need to be rude to simply say no. It's very simple to do it. "I'm sorry but I need to say no to this request." You don't have to explain yourself to strangers. If it makes you feel better, when you say no to a friend, you can add that unfortunately now is not a good moment because you have something else to do. People will understand because they have been in similar situations. And anyone who doesn't understand is not worthy of your self-sacrifice.

If you would like to say no but just don't know how, here's an exercise that will help you. When you have a little spare time to develop your skills, make up different scenarios in which people ask something of you and then try to find a polite way to turn them down. Write these answers down.

How to overcome the feelings of guilt and shame?

People who experienced some kind of childhood trauma often feel guilt, shame, and regret more intensely. But those who didn't have very shocking, traumatic experiences can feel devastated by these emotions too. Shocking or milder but repeatedly bad experiences create negative neural pathways in the brain and can skew perception.

The good news is that you can use neuroplasticity to change your thoughts. Your focus enforces your neural pathways and you can get stuck. If you focus on what you did wrong, guilt and shame will occur. If you focus on what others did to you, you'll feel resentment and anger. By shifting your focus to the lessons you learned thanks to shameful or angering events, you'll strengthen your wise, self-reflective, and positive side.

If you can't get past the shame and guilt, you'll consume your mental resources recycling and reliving your pain. Choose to stop ruminating on the sarcastic sentence your mom told you or the awkward handshake you had. Stop reliving those memories over and over.

There is a practice for this in cognitive behavioral therapy, a very easy one. It's called STOP (or STOPP, or Stop!, or simply thought stopping). Whenever you notice your thoughts going crazy, and guilt- or shame-driven anxiety or blame-driven anger arises in your body, say this word out loud: "STOP." It's necessary to say it out loud instead of just thinking about it, because by talking you involve your different senses. Rumination happens in your mind but saying something like STOP out loud surprises and interrupts the brain. Say STOP as many times as you find it necessary, until you feel that the rumination has indeed stopped.

You can boost this exercise with a pinching exercise. If saying STOP doesn't help or you feel self-conscious saying it as there are other people around, you can try to pinch one of your hands with the other. This practice introduces a different sense into the game than the previous one—touch versus auditory senses—but it works the same way: It disrupts your mental monologue.

The blame cycle

There is another, equally dark side of feeling guilt and shame. It can perpetuate a blame cycle. When we feel that we are under a verbal attack, we often react with defensiveness. One of the most common defenses is offense, and one of the most common offenses is blame. Even if we are the injured party, blaming the other person outright won't help our cause. It's better to not engage in a blame game. This can be frustrating to read right now because we may rightfully want the person who hurt us to feel guilty. But if this person hurt us on purpose out of malice, he or she will seldom accept blame. If our feelings were hurt by the other due to general carelessness or a misunderstanding, throwing the rock back will create further tension.

The attention might divert from us, and before we know it the other party will start acting as the offended one—we'll feel cornered into starting to apologize even though we felt offended first. This can further create a sense of shame or guilt in us. After all, we indeed used blame as a weapon. We might think that blaming others will defend or protect us but, in fact, it just ruins our cause and turns us into a counter-perpetrator.

When a conversation ends up with us apologizing even though we felt we were the one who was offended first, we may feel intense anger and disappointment. We may not think about the events constructively, trying to look at the mistakes made on both sides. We may just feel depressed, dominated, and defeated as we can see the other party getting away without taking responsibility for the pain he or she caused us. We may even feel confusion, thinking that we deserved this and we are the one at fault.

You are not at fault. However, If you were using blame as a communication tool, it's not surprising that you didn't get the results you wanted. Guilt trips never bring good results for either party. Blaming "invites" guilt in. What can you do instead?

I must highlight here that if you are under real danger, someone is threatening your physical safety, is emotionally abusive and toxic to you on purpose, what I'm about to say as an alternative to blame doesn't apply in your case. You should reach for immediate help calling 911, or any other social services in your area that can help you be safe. Blaming is an even worse weapon to use when you face someone unpredictable, aggressive, or abusive. A person who uses these tools of intimidation on you is not a stable, healthy person. Therefore, expecting a stable, healthy response is futile.

Keep that in mind. If they had your best interest in mind, they wouldn't try to be intimidating with you in the first place. They are not necessarily bad people, but they have problems (for example, alcoholics, drug addicts, etc.) that may need to be dealt with by a professional. Your safety comes first.

If you are not in any real danger, difficult interactions that elicit shame and guilt and trigger blame as a response can be handled mindfully. Being hurt but keeping our composure is indeed one of the hardest things in life. We have this natural urge to flee, fight, or freeze (the fight-or-flight response) when we feel under attack. Blaming can bring the opposite result of what we may expect. Keeping silent will make us hold onto grudges and feel powerless. If you hold onto and carry these grudges for too long, their weight will prevent you from moving forward. Also, guilt and shame will stay with you.

Here is how can you handle a shame or guilt trip in the future.

1. Focus on what you're feeling instead of what the other person is doing. For example, someone tells you something that makes you

feel ashamed like "You shouldn't eat more cookies." when you're out eating with friends. Instead of attacking this person for making you feel ashamed, just focus on your feelings. Say "That observation made me feel ashamed." instead of "You are so inconsiderate for saying that. Especially in front of others. You made me feel terrible."

Can you find the blame in the second sentence? It's clearly directed towards the other person. The first sentence on the other hand focuses on the behavior of the person, not the person itself, plus your personal emotions.

2. Try to understand the intentions of the other person. Now that you successfully saved both of you from the blame cycle, try to understand why the person told you what

they said. Don't assume deliberate malice behind their words instantly. Say "I wonder why you said that to me. What was your intention?" instead of "You were out of line to say that to me. It's malicious."

It might turn out that the person had good intentions, trying to help you in an awkward way to help you keep your diet, for example, and stepped on your toes at the wrong time when you were already annoyed with yourself for ruining your diet.

3. Take ownership of your feelings and then explain what went wrong on your side. Try to set some new rules for future reference. "I appreciate your concern for my diet. I already felt lousy about myself for having so little self-control. You held a mirror in front of me, which made me annoyed and even more

ashamed. Next time I'd appreciate if you could remind me of my dieting goals in private, not in front of others." This way you aren't blaming them—you took responsibility for your feelings, admitting that the other person stepped on a toe that already hurt, and offered an alternative for this other person.

4. The other person may or may not take this kind of problem-solving well. That's out of your control. But generally well-intentioned people will take your request in stride. If they keep themselves to your request, in this case not mentioning your diet-sabotaging behavior in front of others, you can consider the talk a success. If they keep on with their hurtful comments, it's time to consider how seriously this person values your request and if they don't, try to distance yourself.

In any case, you can have peace of mind knowing that you did the right thing—the problem didn't escalate, and you can choose how to manage the other person's insensitivity in the future.

Nipping shame and guilt in the bud through effective and non-blaming communication is a great strategy. But what about old wounds? Shaming and guilt triggering experiences you had in the past but you still couldn't get over. Try to recall a few grudges that you have, either for picking a fight about a pain and coming out on the losing end, or not picking a fight and feeling overpowered.

1.

2.

3.

"Holding" or "carrying" grudges imply not only a mental but also a physical heaviness. They can make your life miserable on so many levels. It's "baggage".

Can you imagine dropping your old baggage? Go back to your list on your grudges and write next to each how you would feel if you let go of them and focused on building your new, stronger, happier self up instead. How would you feel if you didn't have these emotional scars in you?

1.

2.

3.

It's not only you, the offended party, who can use the tool of blame. The offender might also use it: Blaming the victim. This is the real shame–guilt triggering combo; when someone says something hurtful to you and then they reinforce it by saying that it's also your fault. One of the most disgusting versions of this combo is blaming rape victims: "You were the one who dressed so provocatively (shame and guilt triggering statement), no wonder you got raped (blame statement)." Of course, this is an extreme case.

There are more subtle ways of shaming and blaming the victim at the same time. I will give you a personal example.

"Your parents raised you to be a spoiled brat, you should have take active steps to change the results of your upbringing a long time ago," someone close to me told me. The sentence unfortunately is true.

Indeed, my parents rose me to be a spoiled brat. I know it, I feel terrible about it—thus getting this directly thrown in my face made me feel very ashamed of myself. This part already is enough to elicit defensiveness as a response. I felt so hurt and I thought it was unnecessary and cruel, given the context that I already admitted that my parents kind of messed me up and I was already spending all my energy towards changing my bad habits.

But what really pierced my heart was the second part of the sentence that washed the first waves of shame over with an even more powerful current of guilt. The worst part was that I believed my accuser had the right to do this to me—after all, he was right about what he said. Being factually right about something and having the right to break someone else's heart out of carelessness or anger are not the same thing.

The problem is that people, when engaging in difficult conversations, focus on proving their righteousness instead of trying to understand the other party and making the other party understand them.

Can you think of anyone who has blamed you? Can you remember what they said and what you felt during and after they placed blame?

1.

2.

3.

Any feelings you still attach to these memories keep you in a dark place and, like gravity, they pull you down. Let go of these negative weights. As these are past events, you can't change them. All you can do is decide to let them go and shift guilt to taking responsibility.

An undeserved sense of guilt and shame can lead you to subconscious self-sabotage. Also, it may keep you in unhealthy relationships. It may keep you from speaking up, make you become someone you do not like or want to be. You may feel like you are the bad person. You will pay a high price for low self-esteem.

Time to get out of this pit.

Think about the patterns of your life. Did you ever stay with someone who wasn't good for you, convinced you didn't deserve, or couldn't find, anyone better? What about making poor choices thinking you didn't deserve more? Think about any decisions you have made based on guilt or shame.

1.

2.

3.

Now think about choices you can make based on freedom. These can be choices you made in the past that made you feel great or choices you'd love to make. Make an exit plan from your toxic relationship, seek out therapy for any guilt, shame, or self-blame issues you may have.

1.

2.

3.

It can be helpful to talk about your shameful and guilty secrets with someone you trust. This can be a nonjudgmental friend, an empathetic, warm professional—releasing shame and guilt is always easier with the help of good people. By finally dropping your shame and guilt baggage, you will boost your confidence and self-esteem. These are characteristics you need to live a healthy and wholesome life.

Chapter 7 - Comparison

Am I good enough? I am sure she will do better than me because she is smarter—oh, why can't I be like her? He is so good with words; everybody is hanging onto his every utterance. I will never attract that much attention.

Familiar thoughts? You can meet them at every corner of the road. But let's look at the fear of comparison—who can invoke it and how you can handle it.

You can meet with the damaging side of comparison from an early age. The most common ones that might affect you are those you get from your parents or close relatives. *Why aren't you helping me more like Susan's daughter? Why aren't you studying as hard as your brother?*

Even if you get over old wounds generated by comparison on the surface—say you become more successful than your "perfect" sister—when you go home and face that you are still not enough for your mother, those deep-rooted scars open up instantly, making you feel little and insignificant. Just as you felt as a child.

What can you do? The common emotion in comparison-related scars is fear. Remember what Yoda said?

"Fear is the path to the dark side. Fear leads to anger. Anger leads to hate. Hate leads to suffering."

Yoda is a Jedi Master. And a Jedi Master knows one or two things about human nature. What are we usually afraid of when we encounter negative comparison? We are afraid of not being enough, of losing love, of being marginalized, of being looked down upon. These are external fears. We can, however, experience some internal fears related to our integrity and adequacy as a human being. And that's a very hard feeling to live with.

People with a healthy sense of self-worth don't allow the destructive power of comparison to take hold on them. They don't take bad behavior personally. Most likely the people who compared you negatively are people in a similar or even worse boat than you. People who spent enough time lacking self-esteem themselves tend to project their bitterness on those around them. Sometimes they are not even conscious of it. They just do it because that's how they were conditioned, or how they were treated before.

Many people are bitter, and can't wait to take a load of bitterness from their back and put it on someone else. They often don't do this consciously or willingly. They are simply so overburdened with negative emotions that all they can think about is "enough, enough, enough". Try to detach from the negative behavior of these people, even if we're speaking about those you love. This is easier said than done, I know.

But think about it. Getting upset and internalizing negatively comparing remarks is futile because the comparison is not really about you. It is about the people who make it: Their fears, rage, and inability to handle their past. As soon as you have a confident and objective picture of yourself, these attacks will bounce off of you.

Discover what's meaningful in life for you.

Oftentimes we compare ourselves to others out of a sense of inadequacy. We are unaware of our own values or if we know what they are, we think that the other person's values are more interesting, cool, important, etc. One way or another, we choose someone else's set of standards to follow.

For example, my partner is all about growing his business. He is an incredible Type A person who always wants to optimize, be more efficient, and maximize profit. He enjoys living this way, loves working on his business that he built from scratch and runs very successfully ever since. Me on the other hand, I love to have my peace of mind. I can work, hard if I need to, but if I don't need to, I prefer to turn my attention onto other things in life, like being calm, doing less, meditating, meeting people, reading, discovering myself, introspecting. For sure I'm not the "get the next million or die trying" type.

But I beat myself up to become one for years because I was so afraid that my partner would not love and respect me otherwise. I also convinced myself that I was in the wrong. His values were much better. He found a way to generate money and takes advantage of that fountain now. Who knows, maybe in two years that source won't provide a living anymore. How bitter would one feel looking back, knowing they could have made much more out of that well with a bit more effort?

So I gritted my teeth, filled my belly with anxiety, and started my fake Type A journey. I felt constantly inadequate as I couldn't do business as well as my partner. I didn't understand what I should do, and frankly I didn't understand *why* I was doing it. The fake identity and value wasn't even for or about me. All I knew was that I didn't want him to judge me or look down on me. Also, that I knew he was a much better and more worthy human being than me.

If the only measurement of worthiness is the ability to capitalize on business, then I was certainly right. But we all know that's not the only aspect that matters in life. Unfortunately, for a period of time, I rejected any other measurement. I compared myself to him obsessively—and I always came out on the losing end. I felt desperate, resentful, and ultimately less. Looking back, the only person who I should have been pissed at was my own self: I put myself into that situation.

I kept seeing myself as a cricket and him the ant. I told myself this story repeatedly. *I'm a cricket, I'm a cricket.* Compared to him, I surely was. I worked seven to eight hours a day—he worked eleven, twelve. I enjoyed our vacations, he had his laptop in his lap. He was always focused on his business first. And I respect him for that. After all, he wasn't untrue to himself. That is *his* major goal at this phase of his life.

But did all this really make me a cricket? Objectively, I worked as well. I had enough income to cover my expenses and put some money into my savings account. Every time I felt my business started to decline a bit, I put more effort in it but once it went well again, and I was in my financial comfort zone, I shifted my focus to other areas of life, and yes, I didn't work sometimes for one or two weeks. Simply because it's not my priority to make more money above a certain level. I read books, hung out with my family, and enjoyed the life for which I was working for instead.

Did this really make me a less worthy person? Of course not. It only made me different. It only meant that business capitalization to me was only a means to some other end. For my partner, it was the end. None of these approaches are wrong. They are different.

But comparing them to each other and deriving self-worth from it is dangerous. It's like wanting to be a tasty apple even though you're an orange. Impossible. The best you can do is to be a great orange, and accept that some will always admire and like apples more—but that doesn't mean that oranges are less good, or worthy.

I learned from destructive comparisons the hard way. Today, fortunately, I can fully embrace my true values. I admire and look up to my partner for his dedication in business but I also know, oh boy, I couldn't be like him. And I shouldn't be. I silently pray and work hard to fulfill my values just as successfully as he fulfills his. And this approach is a much more constructive and powerful one.

Bottom line, find what's meaningful and powerful to you. Make choices and decisions in your life that you believe are right for you.

Discover your strengths.

In order to be able to narrow down what can give the most meaning to you, you need to know your strengths. The problem of comparison here arises because usually we compare our weaknesses with other people's strengths. We compare our gray Monday afternoons with someone else's Saturday night highlight. Flip this mentality around. Start to focus on your strengths.

When we are able to identify our strengths, we'll feel more confident and competent. Also, by knowing our strengths, we can appreciate other people's strengths, too—we can use comparison in a constructive way and grow. Remember, once I found my meaning and my strength in it, my partner became a source of inspiration, not intimidation.

When you see what you're good at, you'll start noticing what others are good at, and you'll stop hating others for it. Conversely, when you don't know or realize what you're good at, your heart will be filled with jealousy, envy, and anxiety. And you won't be envious only over people who do the same thing as you, you'll feel poorly about everyone who is more successful than you are. Once you discover and learn to focus on your strengths, your angle of comparison will shrink to your field of expertise. You won't compare yourself to apples anymore, if you are an orange. Only other oranges.

Take a moment to think about your top five strengths. If you wish to do a deeper dig on your strong points, first write down what you think your top 5 strengths are.

1.

2.

3.

4.

5.

Then ask three people closest to you to describe what your top 5 strengths are. Compare the four lists. Additionally, for extra cost, you can take a paid online survey like CliftonStrengths to get an unbiased report about yourself. (I don't have any affiliation to this company, I just happened to take this test and it was useful to me. You can choose some of the free tests online. However, I can't recommend any, as I didn't try them.)

It is extremely empowering and a big boost to your confidence having your strengths out on paper in front of you. With the help of your friends and strength-finding tests, you can add qualities to your list you didn't even think about—but now you may rightfully feel that these are your strengths, too. Maybe you can get a list of up to twenty qualities that are considered your strengths—not only by you but also other people and sources.

When you consciously recognize some strengths of yours, even those that you wouldn't have come up with alone, you can start using them better. Anyone who goes in-depth on developing their strengths will see improvement in their life.

Have real conversations with people.

One major reason why comparison triggers fear and shame today is a lack of honest communication between people. We don't open up about our honest fears, lacks, flaws—and others also try their best to hide theirs.

Let me illustrate this with a funny story.

I went to a dinner one night at my friend's house. The house was sparkling clean, the food looked picture-worthy and tasted amazing. We had a good time and I invited them to come to my house next; I will make dinner for them instead. I didn't even leave their house when I already started comparing my dining room to theirs, the level of cleanliness of my house, how much effort I would have to put in to clean it at least as well as their place seemed to be. "They live in such cleanliness, they'd judge if I kept my washed dishes on the dish rack all the time." Not to mention the food... when on earth could I cook something like that? Maybe I should just buy it. But what if they ate at the place I'm about to buy the food from, and they realize my treachery?

Long story short, I felt overly stressed by the comparison rabbit hole I entered. But it happens, right? I'm sure many people can relate. The big day came and I was cleaning excessively. I took the trouble to order and pick up food from the other end of the city to minimize the chances of my cooking deception being unmasked. By the time my guests arrived I felt exhausted, and neurotic about everything and the need for it all to be perfect. After the pleasantries were exchanged, and they properly appreciated my sparklingly clean home and amazing food, they asked if I was okay, as I looked unwell.

I felt terribly guilty and, as I'm a preacher of honesty, I decided this was the time for it. I told them how frightened and envious I felt about their sparklingly clean home and posh food, and I worked myself up to keep things up with them. I had been cleaning all day, I put away my dishes and instead ordered food from a restaurant as I'm a lousy cook. *I'm very sorry, but right now I just feel exhausted.*

To my surprise, my friend broke out in a nervous smile. She confessed to me that she felt the same way before I came to their house. She has two young children and usually there is a crazy mess in the house—she was ashamed because of it, so she cleaned because *she* thought that *I* would judge her. She also ordered the food and was equally anxious about my verdict on the dinner hosted by her. How amazing! How silly! And yet, how common...

We listen to an assumption we have about the other person and try to transform our life to fit the expectations we think they have about us. We put up a façade that perpetuates a similar response in the other person. And the cycle of insecurity and inauthenticity grows and grows.

There is a bigger question behind this issue, though, than why we want to keep up with the Joneses. Namely, why do we think that the way we are and live is unacceptable and will be judged? Why is fakery a better option? Why can't we accept that look, that this is how we live day by day? I have dishes on the rack and sometimes books hanging around in random places, and my yoga mat is out 24/7. Why is that so shameful?

How good of a friend is someone who will question our worth as a person based on something like that? Or based on how we dress, how many books we read, how much money we have, what car we drive, or what emotional pain we carry?

I'm not alone with these questions. I bet you also asked some of them already. How about asking them of our friends? Of strangers? What if we got to know people, their real, honest side? What if we discovered that they are just as terrified of being judged as we are?

When you study other people's lives and their pain you'll realize that we're much more alike than we believe, and it's not only you who has problems. Shame and fear generated by comparison instantly disappears once it's called by its name and another person confirms its existence. As Brené Brown said, "Shame can only live in isolation. Once it is shared, it loses its power."

Three ways of healthy comparison.

We can compare ourselves with others in three directions. First, we can compare ourselves with people who are better than us. Second, with people who do worse than us. Third, with people who are on the same level as we are. Each of these forms of comparison can help us if we use them well.

If you compare yourself to the best-performing worker at your firm, you'll feel inadequate, and not good enough. However, if you make a switch and start to look at this kind of comparison as an opportunity for growth, you may find skills in that other person that you currently lack but you can cultivate. You can aim to become better at your job by learning the skills of this person who already does better than you in that field.

When you compare yourself to someone who does worse than you, it can give you temporary peace of mind. For example, if you compare yourself to the worst worker at your company, it may make you feel better about yourself. You're not the worst, but this observation won't make you any better either. The point of downward comparison serves a constructive purpose if you use it to compare your current performance with your past performance. "One year ago I was where they are, and now I'm here. I made great progress, and I'm grateful I learned this and that. It's a good checkpoint to see how far I've come and stop for a moment to be grateful for myself."

Horizontal comparison, when you compare yourself with someone on your level, can trigger a sense of competition. If you use this extra energy to improve yourself and become better for your sake, that's constructive. If you use this energy to defeat, humiliate, or surpass the other person, it's destructive. Make your improvement about you, not the other person.

Positive comparisons can be helpful, but negative comparisons always damage your self-esteem. A positive comparison is when you compare yourself to a person with qualities you admire if it challenges you to improve yourself. Negative comparison, on the other hand, evokes self-loathing, envy, and bitterness. It happens when you compare yourself to someone who has something you don't and you feel bad about it instead of challenged.

If you're really dedicated to getting rid of the negative aspects of comparison, do the following exercise:

Take a piece of paper and write down all of the bad comparisons that haunt you. Put on paper all the thoughts and actions that are a direct consequence of comparing yourself to someone else negatively.

1.

2.

3.

Think about how A-B-C comparisons make you feel. Document every thought and feeling.

For example, if you want to have a relationship for a long time, and your best friend lives in a happy relationship which makes you envious, find out what you feel exactly and why it makes you feel that way. Notice your motivations and try to turn it into a positive cycle: For example, you can try to make notes on what your friend does that makes their relationship work. What are the qualities of your friend that keep their relationship so harmonious? Are they a good listener? Do they respect their partner's boundaries? Are they involved in mutual growth?

Learn from them rather than resenting their happiness in a repressed silence. Speak about your feelings with your friend, explain to them how you feel and seek understanding. These actions might not bring you closer to fulfilling your wish—having a relationship—but neither will unexamined and unhandled envy. Focusing on learning good relationship skills will help you a great deal when Cupid finally finds you.

When you become truly aware that comparing yourself negatively to others doesn't help you, you can be open to looking for replacement thoughts. Practicing gratitude, for instance, is a good thought replacement for negative comparison. Say thanks for the gifts that you do have, all those unique strengths that only you can excel in. Shift your focus to see the good in your life. There are plenty, and you'll find them once you stop being busy comparing yourself with others.

Keeping a gratitude journal is a written way of gratitude. Written things stay visible in the long term while thoughts fly away. It is helpful to secure your self-acknowledging thoughts on paper. It is also a great reminder of your strengths that you otherwise might take for granted. Write in your journal every night three to five things you feel grateful for: Things you got done, places you visited, connections you had. Focus on being grateful for them.

Idealizing another human is unrealistic anyway. Everybody is human, and therefore fallible. You can create a personal cult around someone, but that person is so perfect only in your head. Perfection is frustrating for sure, but the exit key for this frustration is in your pocket.

The world is not a "one versus seven billion" race. It is a one-person race: You against yourself. There is no one you have to be better than, than who you were yesterday. Be 1% better than the day before.

What to do when others compare us negatively?

Negative opinions get stuck in our mind deeper and longer than positive things. It is human nature. It happens to everybody, not just with those who have issues with confidence. Criticism drags us down, haunts us—so it's natural we do our best to avoid these situations. And here we fall into the trap that I call the pleasing spiral.

To avoid criticism we try to fulfill everybody's expectations, do our best in every area of life... we are like a chameleon that has to change color every hour. We don't even remember what our natural color is anymore; we don't know what our self-fulfillment would look like or what we enjoy most in life.

It doesn't matter how well we fake it—how well we learn to blend in—we will still be a gray chameleon amongst wolves. If they want to find a mistake in us, they will. Sometimes, despite your great zeal, we evoke the opposite effect than expected: We get criticized and we feel even more hurt than if we stayed true to ourselves.

Don't work so hard to fulfill others' expectations. The only person's requirements you can fully satisfy are yours. And even that's a hard task. Interestingly, if you are in alignment with your values and act on them with integrity, people won't find so many "mistakes" in you either. They'll rather see you as a role model of self-respect.

To establish a safe base where you can build your confidence, surround yourself with confident, thankful, positive people who practice gratitude in their lives. You are the mish-mash of the five people you spend the most time with, they say. Spend quality time with people who already are similar to who you'd like to be. The more time you spend with them, the more genuinely confident, thankful, and positive you will become.

Don't fall for marketing tricks.

This is the superficial level of comparison-related pain, but it can be quite a sharp one, so let's take a look at it.

Understand that marketers fan the flames of inadequacy by profession. One of their most powerful tools to sell their products is to generate jealousy and envy in your heart. "Look, the Joneses have the newest carpet tassel cleaner! They have the cleanest carpet tassels in the neighborhood! Want to be cool? Buy this product and clean your carpet tassels just like the Joneses!"

Marketers can trigger us to desire the wildest things, especially if someone else already has it. The drive to keep up pushes us to great lengths to get the marketed tool for ourselves.

"If you get this deodorant, you'll be sexy and women will stick under your armpit like a fly trapped in a spider web, right?" Ugh.

But we fall for such stupid ideas nine times out of ten. Be aware. Don't fall prey to these tactics. Recognize them and avoid them. Ask yourself all the time:

Do I really need this object? How will MY life benefit owning this object? Does a clean carpet tassel really make me happy or define me? Will a deodorant turn me into Brad Pitt?

If you're honest, chances are high that your answer will be NO for all these questions. There are important objects that can improve our lives, but usually we end up buying those without any marketing mojo. We know we need them, so we go and buy them. Not because someone else has it, but because we personally need it. End of story.

Be someone who is the trend setter, not the follower. Deep down you already know what it is you were born to be, and you also know what you weren't meant to be. Become the person you would like to follow.

Chapter 8 - The Destructive Power of Judgment

Judgment is part of our life. It is coming from everywhere every minute, every day. But we also dispense it; we make judgments all the time. Our decisions are often judgments. It is useful, sometimes even essential to make judgments. When you start your day by picking a dress to wear, when you select the person you'll sit next to on the bus, when you choose the café to bring your friend to, when you choose a partner to live your life with—all these decisions include a judgment on your part. You do it, others do it. Judging is an indispensable part of living in a society.

Judgment gets nasty when people start obsessing on what others might think about them all the time, or they judge with ill intentions. Judgment with ill intentions invites the fear that they will be also judged with ill intentions. While we might be okay with dispensing such judgments, no one wants to be on the receiving end of it.

Remember this: People will always find a reason to judge if they wish. I saw a picture once that showed a couple having a donkey and two other people badmouthing them.

In the first picture, the couple is walking next to the donkey—*how stupid, they have a donkey and they are walking instead of riding*.

In the second picture, both of them are sitting on the donkey—*poor animal, what an overload*.

In the third picture, only the man is riding the donkey—*what a jerk, he lets his wife walk*.

And in the fourth the woman is on the donkey—*haha, we see who's wearing the pants.*

We have to accept that we will never be able to live up to everybody's expectations. If an unfair judgment hits us when we are building our self-esteem, we need to stand firm and learn to detach from it. Especially if there is no justification for or lesson in the judgment.

What can you do to process it? Evaluate. Consciously analyze your feelings toward that judgment. Why did it bother you? Did it contain any truth? If so, work on that part of yourself. Drift from the intention of pleasing your judges to the genuine wish of improving yourself. If you find the judgment was unfair and inaccurate, remain calm, remind yourself of your values, and just put the judgment in your "bananas" drawer and move on.

Now let's flip the coin, and see the other side.

How prejudiced are you? You know the saying, what goes around comes around. Try to avoid making the mistake that you hate having people do to you. Everybody has a first impression, that's normal. But make sure to dig deeper before jumping to conclusions, and you judge a person harshly and prematurely.

It is harmful, indeed truly damaging, to badmouth, or give a contemptuous glance to somebody before you know what's under the surface. *Why does he or she smell? Why does he or she have such a sorrowful glance?*

It is so easy to say to a girl who wears a lot of makeup that she is a whore, or to assume the boy in the hoodie is a criminal ready to attack. You don't know their stories. Maybe the girl was living under the pressure of maximalist, always-perfect parents who never cared about her and she is trying to gain their attention. Or the boy is regularly beaten by his drunken step-parent and is just trying to hide his bruises. Being purely judgmental won't help anyone, including you.

How to keep under control your natural inclination to judge others.

First accept that you're not that special for having knee-jerk judgments. Everybody does it, everybody has hurt someone else by judging prematurely. You're not alone in this. Don't beat yourself up too much.

What you can do now is consciously make the decision of being more accepting and inclusive—try your best to make snap judgments with less intensity. What I mean by this is that when you notice yourself having a natural snap judgment, stop for a second and think: Why do I feel this way about this person? Why do I feel so strongly about this situation? Why does this matter to me?

Don't attack, ask. Don't snarl, smile. Don't blame, be understanding.

Keeping in mind and living by these three simple sentences will not only help you become a better person, it will also teach you how to be a fairer judge. The same rules apply when you are on the other side: Being the judged. *Don't attack, ask. Don't snarl, smile. Don't blame, be understanding.*

Why should you do this when you're on the receiving end of judgment? Because you know better now. If someone still operates from the darker side of judgment, it doesn't mean the best thing you can do is descend to that person's "level".

It's better to try to elevate that person to a better way of doing and looking at things. Lead by example.

For example, if someone tells you that you're bad at communication, there are two ways you can react.

Attack:
You'll tell that person where to stick it and that you're great at communication. They are the one bad at communicating, that's why you can't communicate with them.

Ask:
I'm surprised that you feel that way. I rarely get this feedback. Why do you think I'm bad at communicating?

It takes a great deal of character not to react badly to a direct criticism such as "You're bad at communicating." However, if you just defend and counterattack, the best you can get out of it is protecting what you already think you know: Your pride in your communication skills. If you're approaching the comment with curiosity you might learn something new.

Smile or snarl:
It helps if you smile rather than snarl at a person who approaches you with hostility. Every human on this Earth ultimately wants connection and dreads rejection. When someone attacks you, they expect some kind of resistance, for you to fight.

Imagine someone's surprise when they get a different reaction. The opposite they expected. That could break their walls of hostility instantly, leaning in to the connection they so wish to get. "I was mean to this person, yet, my opinion is important enough to them to ask me about it. They aren't attacking me. They're smiling. I'm safe to let my guard down."

Blame:

"Well, if you feel that I'm a bad communicator, you should tell it to me in a different form than such a direct attack. You are hostile and that makes me not want to talk with you."

Understand:

"I know how difficult it is to tell a criticism to someone. You must have felt a lot of stress about calling me out. Why was it so important to you to tell me this?"

First, try to understand why this person called you out on your bad communication skills. Why do they feel that way? Do they feel ignored, not listened to, not heard, or insulted by something that wouldn't seem insulting to you?

Approach them with the goal of trying to get to an understanding, not a goal to tell them how much they hurt you. Interestingly, once someone feels heard, they'll much more likely listen to you and hear your hurt. They might even apologize for the raw manner in which they attacked you.

And hey, not as a last point, you proved them wrong: You do communicate well.

When flaws are good.

Reflect on how your flaws helped you in your life. All your flaws can be values at the right time, in the right proportion, and in the right situation. In my case, for example, I can be very aggressive in pursuing my "survival". I can go over people from time to time for that, and objectively this is not a good trait. But without this trait there was no way I could have ended up living a good life where I have the freedom to help others. My aggressiveness led me through adult hardships at the age of fifteen, sixteen, living alone, without parents or much money.

This observation applies to judgments as well. You don't only judge in a negative way, but also in a positive. When you choose your friends, your life's partner, your education, your career, you need to make value judgments. It is not a flaw if you use judgment in a way that makes your life happier and more complete.

That's why it is so important to know your values, and make judgments for your benefit, but not at the expense of others.

Don't confuse external judges with the one living between your own two ears. You can be your greatest critic. Sometimes you don't even need others. Your mind can create a loop where you imagine someone judging you, but in reality you are judging yourself. Nobody ever will judge you as harshly as you judge yourself in moments of self-contempt. Collecting the courage to move past your negative automatic criticism is often the greatest challenge you'll face on the way to overcome fear of judgment.

Self-criticism can be your friend and your enemy, just like all of your "flaws". It is your enemy when it prevents you from living fully, but it is a friend when you use it for self-reflection. It gives you clarity on where you have to improve.

Without healthy self-criticism, you'd never improve. Finding the areas where you can improve will turn you into a professional instead of a conceited amateur. If you feel that you're not good enough in a craft after one month or one year of practice, you're probably right. Search for the areas where you can improve and grow. This is what it means to have healthy self-criticism.

If, however, you constantly tell yourself that you'll never be good at anything because you're a loser, a quitter, so on and so forth, that's not healthy self-criticism. That's self-sabotage. This type of negative self-talk brings you down and keeps you there. Did you recognize any of those phrases? Do you say stuff like this to yourself? Turn those thoughts into constructive self-criticism like this:

Negative self-criticism:
I will never be a good swimmer because I'm uncoordinated.

Constructive self-criticism:
How can I improve my coordination skills to become a better swimmer?

Negative self-criticism:

I will never be as good as Jane at copywriting.

Constructive self-criticism:

How can I improve my copywriting skills? I should ask Jane what she did to get so good.

Don't let your own self-judgment prevent you from living the life you deserve. Use self-criticism to your benefit by turning negatives into constructive ideas and goals.

Chapter 9 – Positive Reinforcement

Wherever you were born, whatever your life path was until now, you have to know one vital thing: The things that have happened to you are absolute determinants of who you can be in the future.

If you think, "I am still not brave enough to step out from the crowd, I still feel fear," that's good. It is good to be afraid of the unknown—at least at the beginning. It's natural. Who becomes a champion? I'll tell you, not the brave ones who run forward deep into the uncharted territory of the enemy. They get slaughtered first. Champions, winners, will be the ones who are cautious, who are led by fear in the beginning, who think through their options, their capabilities, their strengths and weaknesses, the threats they could be facing, and discover the unknown territory step by step.

Champions are not perfect, untouchable, or invincible. They are those who fail tremendously but get up, admit their mistakes, learn from them, and go on. They might not win in the first round, but they persist and eventually win.

"If someone else can do it, why can't I?"

This is the question I ask myself every time I lose faith in myself. It makes me challenge my limiting beliefs. This motto may sound strange because it is based on a comparison, which we know is not always helpful. But this type of approach is the exception that empowers the rule. Here we don't measure ourselves by others, but by success itself. We can rephrase it as: "Success has been made in this field, it exists so it is reachable—therefore I can and will reach it."

Among others, this sentence helped me write my first book. Being a writer makes you face a lot of fears. What if nobody will like my book? What if I am not good enough to give value to others? These are the fears I had. I had my one-day paralysis, then I continued writing.

And here you are with my book in your hands, and I will be very happy if I can add any value to your life. Staying positive is not easy. It is a matter of decision. You also can decide to stay negative and to be a victim. How do you decide?

Be grateful every day.

If you decide to stay positive, start it in the morning. When you wake up, start your day with gratitude.

You have so many reasons. Be grateful that the sun is shining. Be thankful that you could open your eyes and a new day full of possibilities awaits you. Don't open your cell phone, don't read the news right after you wake up. Start your day with meditation, yoga, a nice mug of coffee in nature instead. You'll feel much happier, balanced, and optimistic.

How to start your day on a positive note is important, but it is just as important to *stay* positive. In this chapter you'll read about techniques on how you can build the habit of staying positive.

Tony Robbins said, "Either you're growing or you're dying." If we give credit to this statement, focusing on growth can help us find meaning in our day-to-day life. Having a meaning won't necessarily make us happy 24/7, but it can make us be more positive and hopeful.

Having a growth mindset won't make your life perfect. Having a positive, hopeful outlook on life won't make negative things vanish. No. You will still have your daily hardships, but your responses will be different, and that's the real change. Confident people seem so amazing because they defeat life's struggles with hopefulness spread on their faces, because they know after the rain there is always sunshine and any hardship is just a natural part of the sequence of events we call life. This doesn't mean that confident people never feel negative emotions, just that their attitude of processing them is better.

People conduct their everyday lives through their habits. Let's align the power of habits to our favor. How? By starting to practice good habits and building them into our daily routines.

What can these habits be?

Morning glory.

When you wake up, start your day with an optimistic thought. It can be the same thought. You can pin it next to your bed to greet yourself with it each day.

Don't focus on what you hate, focus on what you love.

Don't hate Mondays, don't hate mornings—even if you do. If you keep on repeating that you hate something, you'll act accordingly. Tell yourself "I love waking up because this will be an amazing day." or "I'm grateful I could wake up so early because this way I have more time for myself." Replace the hateful thought with something that is actually true. Try to find something that you can appreciate even in your misery and focus on that.

There is power in persuasive negative or positive words—whether others say them to you, whether you tell them to yourself. If you can't tell yourself anything but hurtful words, you'll start acting accordingly. People like to be in accordance with who they believe they are.

If you start believing good things about yourself, you'll start acting to validate them, and vice versa. It's important to tell things to yourself that you can truly believe. If you are objectively overweight, for example, telling yourself you're thin won't help you out. You can do two things in this case: Either you enforce your perseverance ("I relentlessly persevere in my quest to lose X pounds.") or you learn to accept yourself honestly as you are ("I'm aware that I'm overweight by X pounds but I'm worthy and lovable.").

Stop complaining. Act.
There is a subtle difference between sharing your struggles with others in the hope of finding some peace and relentlessly complaining. This subtle

difference is in the actions you take after you told your story; namely, now that you have identified your problem, what will you do to solve it? Some people get stuck in the rut of complaining. All they do is go around, meet friends or strangers, and tell them their story. They may feel better for a little while, but the problem they are complaining about won't be solved.

Let's take the example of infidelity.

Erick's long-term girlfriend cheated on him. They broke up, which made Erick feel miserable, dishonored, and alone. He felt that a great injustice happened to him. It was a normal reaction for him to go and tell his misfortunes to his friends, spreading out his pain. He felt heard, and his friends offered him support.

However, one year passed and the only thing Erick could talk about was his unfaithful ex, detailing his misery as if it happened yesterday. He couldn't sympathize with his friends who lived in happy relationships: "Well, I love how naïve you are. It's coming. Cheating is coming for you, too."

Of course, no one likes to have such shadows cast upon their happiness. People started distancing themselves from Erick, who was unable to understand why, and he felt that even his friends "cheated" on him.

What could Erick have done differently? After his natural grieving period, Erick decided that enough is enough. Why should he suffer because of someone who didn't want him? Why should he develop this "cheated guy" identity? He really wanted to avoid the experience of being cheated in the future and in order to do this he had to figure out why he was cheated on in the first place.

Was it something about his behavior? Was it something about his ex's past, family background, self-esteem? Both?

He went to therapy where he uncovered a more objective reality. He stopped seeing himself as the victim and his ex as the perpetrator. He learned to see the dynamic that led to that hurtful conclusion. He accepted his part in the matter and started to work hard to improve himself as a person and as a future partner. He took responsibility for his actions, and his life. He wasn't a victim anymore, he was empowered, and he talked to his friends about the amazing journey of self-understanding he was on. His friends were admiring his courage, vulnerability, and strength to have such an honest look on himself.

Soon, he found a new partner who deeply appreciated him for who he was. Today Erick looks at his cheating experience as one of the best things that happened to him, as without it he would have never stepped onto the path of deeper self-understanding and change which led him to his current happiness.

Learn to find happiness within.

If you always expect somebody else to entertain you, to compliment you, to cheer you up to become positive, you will never feel safe enough to be happy. You know that the key to your positive mood depends on others. You'll be in a dependent situation, exposed to others' mood and goodwill.

The purpose of empowering people is to add something to your general positive attitude, not to establish it. If you are happy, they make you more joyous. If you are angry, or a genuinely negative person, positive people who try to make you happier will just make you even angrier and more resentful. "How can they be so annoyingly cheerful? I'm sure they're faking it."

Staying on the mentally sunny side is more of a choice than a natural state of mind. In fact, humankind is wired to be negative. Our ancestors had to be on their guard 24/7. They always expected the worst, and they were right to do so. Around every corner there could be a tiger or an inimical tribe to take their lives. As centuries passed, we kept this imprinting. Negativity is still a more natural state to be in. If you feel that you instinctively give a negative response most of the time, embrace it. There's nothing wrong with you. It means that your basic instincts work well.

Being negative now and then is normal and natural.

It's also important to acknowledge, however, that there are no tigers and inimical tribes around anymore, and we have a choice in how to react to our negative emotions.

Having constructive, positive reactions requires everyday mindfulness. Staying calm and reacting well in the face of intense negative emotions can become a habit eventually, but it can never become such an innate, elementary instinct as negativity. Expecting yourself to stay positive after a brief practice is not a realistic wish. Expecting to stay positive after ten years of practice is not realistic either. Expecting to avoid negative thinking entirely is also not realistic.

Becoming wired to positivity is like having an incurable disease. You have to learn to live with it. Living with positive mentality is just like an incurable illness. It requires you to take a pill each day to keep yourself afloat. In positivity's case, this pill is gratitude, happy thoughts, and acceptance.

Keeping yourself on the positive side is a lifelong commitment. There is no easy way around it, but the more you practice the things that make you feel positive, the easier it will become. It will become a routine.

When should you start your positive practices? Now. Now is always the right time to make a change. Not tomorrow, not Monday, not next month... if you want something badly, do not hesitate. Want to start a diet? Start it now. Do you want to stop smoking? Put down that cigarette in your hand. Want to become more positive? Tell yourself three things you feel grateful for. Now, now, now. Time-wasting kills action. Start practicing now.

Practice.

All that you've read requires diligent and committed practice. Nobody will pass all the tests they take the first time. The first time you might fail, and the second, and even the eighth. Even if you focus very hard, you might still fail to act to your standards occasionally. That's okay, that's natural. Acknowledge it, accept it, and keep practicing.

Failing for the 10th time is a great achievement—it means you tried nine more times after the first failure. Don't give up! It is not enough to practice just a few times, you have to be persistent. There will come a moment when you realize what you practice doesn't require as big a focus anymore because it has become a habit. You won't even remember the last time you didn't succeed in keeping up your spirit.

Chapter 10 - Set Your Goals

Here is the opportunity in your life: You created it, therefore you can change it. You are the designer and implementer of the life you always wanted to live. There is no implementation without a design. What would you like to implement? You cannot have your dream life if you don't know what it looks like. First you need a very clear vision of what you would like to do, achieve, reach, or realize.

You will need a goal built up step by step. Smaller steps in the beginning—you don't want to miss any foundational stones. In the planning session, imagine yourself being the person you want to be, doing the things you want to do. Think about what would make you fulfilled. To answer this question more easily, think back to what made you happy in the past. Take your time to find your values, happy places—within you and around you—and have them as a crystal clear vision.

The things that made me happy:

1.

2.

3.

How to set your goals.

To start the implementation of your (newfound) goals, take out a piece of paper. Write down your main life goal in detail, who you want to become, what you want to achieve, and what kind of people you would like to have around you. See your ideal self, your ideal life, vividly.

Pin this paper on your wall, read it every day. Look at your dream plan, meditate about it as if it was already yours. Visualize it, feel it, love it. And trust it is meant for you.

Let me illustrate this process with a trivial, capitalistic example. The idea of online shopping lies on the same principle. You found your dream product on an online shop; it has a price and a delivery date. This is the object of your desires, not something you can easily access and take home immediately. But you want this product so you pay for it now, and know it will arrive at some point.

Of course, you have your doubts—what if the online shop does not make the delivery? You've paid in advance and you risk getting nothing. Better not to buy it, you may think, and instead stick to the safe and secure product at the mall that you can buy right now but won't fulfill your true desires. The item at the mall isn't *exactly* what you wanted, but it's a sure thing. However, you will feel it is average, and you will be unhappy about your purchase, even feel the price you paid was not worth it.

There's always a risk, but some go for the real deal. They order their dream product online, they pay its price in advance. They know they have done everything correctly to get it. A period of waiting follows, and the anticipation will give every day a feeling of excitement because they know what they most want is going to arrive soon.

Fulfilling your dream goal is not totally the same. It is not enough to just figure out what you want and then just wait for it to happen. You have to put in a lot of effort to reach your goal—as though you'd be the buyer and the delivery guy of the online shop at the same time. If you can believe in an online store, why shouldn't you believe in yourself?

In my life, I've often wondered what the difference is between those who achieve success and those who don't. Some people are like King Midas: Everything they touch becomes gold. Some people don't succeed even if the gold is put directly into their hands. If you take two people with the same level of innate qualities, same opportunities, who grew up under the same conditions, what is it that makes them so different?

Their attitude.

One's attitude can make the biggest difference. It is the only "weapon" that is always within your control and does not depend on anything or anyone else; it is completely up to you. You set its boundaries, and if you choose, it can be limitless. The key is that you cannot have a different life with the same attitude you've always had.

How do you change your attitude?

First, learn to love yourself. Without self-love, you will never be able to believe 100% in yourself. You simply won't consider yourself worthy of those gifts of life you're aiming for. Self-love is essential. If you did the exercises in this book, you have a clearer picture of who you are and why you're a worthy person. I hope you knew it before, but if you didn't, now you know. Accept your strengths and weaknesses.

Why is self-love important?

Because you can't give something you do not have. You can't devote yourself to a goal if you hate the person you're trying to reach that goal for. If you don't love yourself, every goal you have will seem undeserved. At some point you'll sabotage yourself. What's more, you won't be able to love somebody else if you do not fully appreciate yourself. You will be moody, insecure, and you will radiate this in your environment. You won't be able to be happy for another's success because your first thought will be jealousy: "When will I have that?" or "When will they celebrate *me* as they do my partner?" Jealousy is a bitter feeling that leads to comparison, anxiety, self-loathing, and sorrow.

If you love yourself, you'll be able to believe in your worth unconditionally. You'll feel that you deserve what you're fighting for, that you can achieve it. Also, you will be happy for others' achievements because they will inspire you. Successful people around you will give you an extra boost. "They did it! I am so proud! I should try it myself. They can advise me how. I am so lucky to have them around!" It sounds different.

Do not build your self-love upon feedback from the outside world. Do not make your self-love dependent on others' opinions. You are worthy, lovable, and respectable even if you don't hear it every day from other people, or worse, if you hear the opposite. "If you live by others' praising, you'll die by their criticism."

Self-confident people interpret feedback as they choose to. If somebody tells you that you will never be able to achieve your goals, you have two options. The first option is to believe these words and give up on them. Your second option is to consider the person who said this to you and notice that they are a person who never fulfilled their goal, and that their statement is not really about you. It is about their own believed incompetence, which they are projecting onto you.

Some might think self-love can easily turn into arrogance. This is not true. Arrogance is just like an inferiority complex, and is the sign of a lack of self-confidence and self-love.

Love yourself, respect yourself, and believe in yourself. Until you do it, nobody else will.

The realization that you wasted your life because of fears, conformism, and excuses is like a sharp blade. Whatever your problems are, you've got this life to live. You won't be able to live anyone else's life. You can only be happy in yours. You can only love this person you are.

Do you think that you're not strong enough to make a difference in your life? Do you think that loving yourself doesn't make a difference? Do you think that small changes can't have big impact? Then you've never been locked with a mosquito in a dark room.

"Aim for the moon. If you miss, you may hit a star." - W. Clement Stone

The decision is yours; it always has been.

Closing Thoughts

It is not enough to try something. Trying is your subconscious making excuses. When you tell yourself you'll try something, you'll automatically allow failure to be an option. Trying means taking a chance halfheartedly, and if it doesn't turn out as expected? Oh well, you told everyone that you were only trying. Do or do not, there is no try. Yoda.

Aim for what you want. Maybe you won't succeed on the first try. In most cases, good things don't happen on the first try. You have to pursue what you want again and again.

A success mentality requires knowledge and confidence in your capabilities. Commit to do your very best. A growth mindset has a greater chance for success. Said by Sun Tzu: Never enter in a battle with the thought of failure. If someone starts something convinced that they won't succeed, they'll probably be right. If someone engages in something convinced of winning, they might still fail the first time, but chances are that at some point they will win. They'll get richer with lessons, at the very least.

Remember: Success comes in cans, failure in can'ts.

It doesn't matter if you have a small dream or an earth-shockingly big, ridiculous, and unbelievable one—there is no such thing as impossible, only lack of focus, inaction, and the self-conviction that impossible exists. If "impossible" truly existed, we wouldn't have people like Albert Einstein, Neil Armstrong, or Elon Musk. They all did something that decades or centuries before was considered to be impossible.

Don't collapse beneath the size of your dream. It is less risky to aim bigger than to aim for mediocrity. There's much more competition in the middle ground. Tim Ferriss said in his book *The 4-Hour Workweek* that doing the unrealistic is easier than doing the realistic. It's quite empty at the top.

Are you convinced that you can't achieve great things? So is 99% of the rest of the world. Everyone aims for the mediocre goals or the easily attainable. The competition is the most significant on that level. Having a mind-blowing goal supplies you with a constant adrenaline rush that gives you the endurance needed to reach it. Mediocre goals, on the other hand, are uninspiring. They won't keep you fueled as much as the big ones, and therefore sooner than later you'll give it up.

Have an honest assessment over your abilities when you have to make a decision. Accept that some things are not meant for you yet. If, for example, you know nothing about chemistry, you can't reasonably aim to become a pharmacist in a year. If you truly wish to become one, however, it's not impossible. That's the end goal. In order to achieve that, you need to have a degree in chemistry first. Your small task goal should rather be to finish your freshman year at a university in this subject. This seems more achievable from today's distance, doesn't it? And, you have all the abilities that are required to complete this task. Some dreams simply require deep study and devotion to achieve success.

If you face a challenge that seems "impossible", ask yourself if you truly want to be successful in this field. Are you ready to put energy in it? Will you be persistent enough about learning the skills, filling the gaps that you need to reach this dream? Would it bring you joy and passion if you devoted time and energy to it? If your answers are all "Hell yeah!" then go for it! Start now!

Every challenge is an opportunity. It is up to you what you make of it. Just make sure to plant those seeds in fertile soil. Even if you don't get the desired outcome—even if you fail a few times—it doesn't mean you didn't get anything worthwhile out of it and it was all a waste of time. You got a lot out of it: You got new information about your current limits, and practice in persistence. If you choose to do something instead of being passive, regardless of the outcome, you are already a winner. Get up and try it again, differently.

Life is too short to live for the sake and recognition of others. Confidence, self-love, and a positive attitude are not age-related. It is never too early or too late to make a change.

You might feel you are climbing the highest mountain, and everything is against you—the odds, your family, your friends. Do not believe anybody who says you are not able to do it, or that it is useless to try. It is never useless to be committed to do better. Change is constant in your life—and if you have to change, by all means, why not for the better?

I wrote this book based on my experiences, what I felt hindered me and boosted me during my path of self-discovery—which is still a work in progress. I wish you all the best with your journey, and I hope you will be able to use some of my advice to get wherever you wish to go.

Along the way, you will make mistakes. Don't worry about them, they are part a part of the deal. Don't give up, be persistent, and have your goals clear in front of you! Remember that everything takes time, so be patient.

Stay true to your heart, stay in the present, and believe that being your best self each day will take you to your desired future!

I believe in you!

Sincerely,

Zoe

Endnotes

---

[i] Kendra, Cherry. What is the Superego? Verywell Mind. 2018.
https://www.verywellmind.com/what-is-the-superego-2795876

[ii] Kendra, Cherry. What is the Superego? Verywell Mind. 2018.
https://www.verywellmind.com/what-is-the-superego-2795876

www.ingramcontent.com/pod-product-compliance
Lightning Source LLC
Chambersburg PA
CBHW052042280426
43661CB00085B/53